BRAMPTON
Then and Now

✶✶✶✶✶

Iain Parsons

Published by
'Netherhay Books',
Far Hills, Capon Tree Road,
BRAMPTON, Cumbria, CA8 1QL
email: ihparsons@aol.com

Printed by Advance Book Publications, Church Road Industrial Estate, Northmoor, Witney, Oxon., OX29 5UH

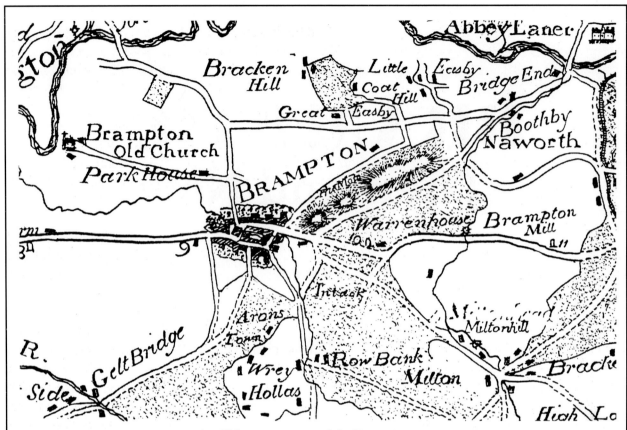

An 18th century map of the Brampton area

There are some places marked on this map which have vanished without trace. One of these is 'Hollas', which stood on Tarn Road just to the south of 'Moss House', but on the opposite side. Another is 'Row Bank', which was on the track from the station that leads down towards the Tarn Road, but doesn't actually reach it. 'Intack', too, has gone – this would have been on what is now Tree Road. 'Park House', on the road to the Old Church, is another property that has not survived. Some of the roads shown have never been converted to metalled highways, others have just disappeared or become footpaths.

CONTENTS

FOREWORD

It seemed only a matter of days after my second book went on sale that people were asking, 'Are you going to do another?' My answer was, 'Yes, if there is a demand and new pictures are forthcoming!' That the demand is there is clear – the books have sold well. Many people from places far removed from north Cumberland, indeed, all over England and several from abroad have bought copies.

Once again, I have been overwhelmed by kindness, co-operation and generosity in the provision of old photographs, postcards and family snapshots, all of which have shown some aspect of the town in days gone by. There have been reminiscences by the score and it is such open-handedness that makes books such as this possible.

Personally, I am thankful that there is such interest in the past life of this small town. Some of the stories in this book are published for the first time. Some people may have heard these tales at their grandparents' knee, but to others, they will be quite new and provide an insight into that very different world in which our ancestors lived.

This is not the place for a lesson in social history, but we should remember just how much life has changed over the past century in respect of the more basic things. We can switch on an electric light – there is no fiddling with a tinder box or Lucifer matches; we pick up a telephone and talk within seconds to someone half a world away; we can turn on the radio or television and receive news from around the globe; we turn on a tap and hot or cold water issues – there is no going to the local pump; we light the gas and we can cook – the stove does not require tending. Supermarkets supply food in or out of season. Unless we were high-born, the bygone way of life was vastly different from the relative ease of today.

So here is another selection of illustrations and observations about Brampton. I hope that there is as much pleasure to be gained as the previous books have provided!

ACKNOWLEDGEMENTS

I feel that I must give some recognition to the people who have helped in any way to the production of this book. In the past, I have not always made a note of the donors of pictures or texts, but this omission has been rectified! If I have missed anyone, I must ask for pardon!

For photographs:

Mr. D. Adams; Mrs. K. Adams, Darlington; Mrs. L. Allason; Mrs. K. Bestwick; Mrs. M. Dalton; the late Mr. C. Dryden; Mrs. M. Findlay; Hon. P. Howard; Mr. J. Howe; Mr. R. Huie; Mr. J. Hunter; Mrs. A. Jeffrey; Mr. J. Lee; Mrs. J. Moorat; Mr. A. Morris; Ms. A. Noble; Mr. Robson, Carlisle; Mrs. G. Simpson; Miss M. Taylor; the late Mr. Watson and Mrs. Worrall, Newark.

For help with text checking:

Mrs. J. Hempstead, Hon. P. Howard, Mr. J. Howe, Mr. J. Lee, Mrs. S. Reynolds, Mrs. S. Ritchie and Mr. W. Wilkinson.

For encouragement:

There are too many people to mention!

For support:

From everyone who purchases the book.

For tolerance:

Hilde Parsons.

THE SANDS and TREE ROAD

The new housing development between the Sands and Tree Road has caused a major change in this area. The open land has been almost covered with houses, with the exception of Jock's Hill itself and, had it not been for strenuous objection, this would have been developed also. The totality of this can be seen in the next few illustrations. The first of these pictures was taken from the top of Jock's Hill in 1956. In the foreground are the Thomlinson Cottages and Corner Cottage, part of the Wilson homes development. In the upper right hand corner can be seen the back of the Sands Cottages. It must have been taken on a Monday – look at the washing on the line!

The second picture in the series is taken from the same viewpoint at the same time, but looking towards Tree Road. Tree Terrace occupies a conspicuous position and the smaller bungalows on the north side of the road can be seen, sitting much lower than one imagines. 'Uplands', now named 'Kara Orchard', is just above the last light roof towards the right, with the Cottage Hospital behind it.

The next picture, taken from The Ridge, dates from 1990 and clearly shows the fields behind the Wilson Homes as 'open' countryside. Tree Terrace can be seen, just to the right of centre.

The second picture, which was taken in April 2002 from a slightly altered viewpoint on the Moat, shows a very different appearance. At the bottom left of the photograph, the Sands Cottages' end wall faces on to Lovers' Lane. The slope of Jock's Hill can be seen on the left of the picture and crammed round its foot are the buildings of the new estate. Even allowing for the masking effect of the trees on the Moat, the jamming in of the houses can be clearly discerned. Unfortunately, this is

Beckside Gardens, May 2000

not the only part of the town where solid infilling has occurred, as in Beckside Gardens. Very little space has been left between the individual dwellings.

A question that was brought to my attention recently was the unusual and atypical size of the houses on both Ridgevale Terrace and Tree Terrace. They are quite unlike anything else we have in the town. The explanation offered is both logical and somewhat unexpected. In the late nineteenth and early twentieth centuries, Brampton was a popular place to spend holidays and people came from distant parts to enjoy the relaxing atmosphere and pure air that the town offered. It is very likely that these large terraces were built to provide lodging houses for the influx of visitors. There is certainly an advertisement for accommodation at Ridgevale Terrace in a 1901 guidebook to the town. It is worth considering the theory that widowed ladies who had fallen on hard times might have offered such facilities. The widows' pensions did not exist and, if the husband had died young or poor, life could be very hard for such women. However, I digress!

There were many rambles that could be taken without too much physical effort – round the Tarn, through the park at Naworth, to Gelt Woods and to the Old Church, to name a few of the more obvious ones. Many guidebooks to the town and its environs were published a hundred years or so ago, all of which included walks and more organised trips by horse drawn carriage. Some of these would be fraught with danger today with the speed and density of motor traffic, but in those far-off days, an encounter with a horseless carriage would be a rare occurrence! Many of the hotels provided horses for the use of their clientele, should they wish to travel further afield.

The Sands, from an old postcard of the early twentieth century.

This very faded postcard on the previous page is almost a 'Cinemascope' view and shows the huge trees that lined the Station Road before the Wilson Homes were built in 1930. The little weighing house that served the coal staithes, mentioned elsewhere in this book, can be seen on the extreme right of the picture. The house next to it is 'Fair Hill'. Faintly, in the distance in the middle of the picture is 'Ridge Valley' and to the left of that are the Earl Grey Cottages. The overall appearance of the Sands has not changed greatly, apart from the few newer houses at the very end of Lanercost Road.

Earl Grey Cottages and the new seat, May 2000.

This photograph is a modern one of the Earl Grey Cottages, which was a public house initially called the 'Wellington' Inn. This lost its licence as a result of Lady Carlisle's temperance campaigns of a century ago. The seat is a new addition to the Sands' scenery, having been erected in 2000, one of several placed in the parish. Behind the car and in the picture below, one can discern the strange wooden 'sculptures', which stand at the bottom of the track leading up to the Moat.

The Sands, May 2002.

A NOW-VANISHED REMNANT OF THE BRAMPTON RAILWAY

The weigh house in the early 1950s

About 200 years ago, a small square building stood in Station Road opposite the end of Tree Road. When the Earl of Carlisle's wagon way was built in 1799 to bring coal to Brampton from Tindale Fell, this was the site of the staithes where the coal was sold. This building was the check-house and later, the weigh house for the coal. It was built of stone, with a hipped roof, fine stone ridges and a central chimney. Until about 1976, it had been used (somewhat appropriately, in view of the transport patterns) as the office for the adjacent petrol station, but room for expansion was needed and it was to be demolished.

Mrs. Joanna Matthews was concerned that this part of Brampton's railway history would be swept away without any trace remaining, but it was arranged with the headmaster of Edmond Castle School that the building would be carefully taken down and re-erected at the school. With the presence of skilled building instructors on the staff, it was felt that this would make an interesting school project. In addition, the little building would be preserved and could be seen by enthusiasts.

The Coal Staithes, Summer 2000.

9

THE ROAD TO LANERCOST

At the very end of the road to Lanercost, where it joins the main Newcastle Road, one of the old town pumps still stands in working order. I am told that the residents of the area preferred this source, even after piped water had been provided, as it was 'much sweeter'. The Sands shelter is in the background.

Below is Ridgevale Terrace, virtually unaltered from one hundred years ago in its overall appearance. The railings have gone, presumably to 'help' the war effort sixty years since, but it is more likely that they were laid somewhere to rust away, as happened to so many such sacrifices. Other

Ridgevale Terrace, Lanercost Road.

changes, such as the shrubs cannot be dated. The signs of horse-drawn traffic, so prominent in early street photographs, can give some indication of the date of a picture by the density of 'coverage', but here there is nothing to guide us. The field on the left, at the end of the terrace now has a row of houses built upon it.

Quarry Beck is the stream that runs down towards the Abbey Mill at Lanercost. This picture, shown on the next page, is a postcard illustration: the stamp was Edwardian. The footpath, which runs from 'Ridgefoot' at Easby Road end, follows the stream through the woods and passes the sawmill at Boothby on its way. In the 1850s, this was owned and run by George Pickering, who was related to the family whose handiwork can be seen every day in the town centre – they were the paviours who set the cobbles. The original sawmill was destroyed by fire a few years ago, but has since been rebuilt.

Quarry Beck

The Old Sawmill at Boothby, as painted by
Harry Close in 1975

The present sawmill, taken in 1998

The restored Abbey Mill

Some may question whether the next few pictures have any right to be contained in a book about Brampton! I have always tried to remain within the parish boundaries and, though it may seem surprising, I have still done so! The 'Bridge End complex' is actually within Brampton Parish, although it is always referred to as 'Lanercost'.

At the end of the path that follows the Quarry Beck is the Abbey Bridge Mill, restored some time ago as a dwelling. The board announcing the name bears the date 1600 on the front.

The Lanercost Temperance Inn, about 1900

The view of the Lanercost Temperance Hotel, another of Lady Carlisle's successes, is probably around 1900, judging from the girls' style of dress. The cycle itself is very early. A similar machine appears in other pictures of the area. Whether the rider is the photographer himself or merely an assistant is unknown.

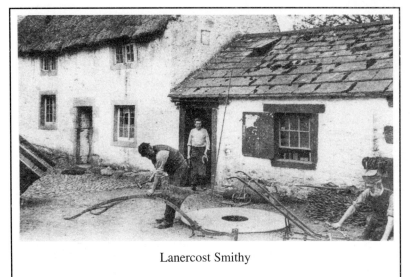

Lanercost Smithy

The old machinery stands outside the smithy, which is shown on the adjoining picture. The circular plinth, for shrinking the metal tyres on to the cartwheel rims can be clearly seen. In addition, there is a dismantled plough, another under repair and a stack of discarded horseshoes. It is interesting to speculate how these were recycled. It is clear that the picture has been carefully posed. The single storeyed building is now long gone, but the thatched one still remains as part of the hotel complex.

The next illustration is also an old postcard and must have been taken from the hill behind the inn, looking across towards the Priory, which can be seen at the extreme left edge of the picture.

The Old Bridge from a picture postcard

Another cyclist appears on this much later picture, taken from the south. The little smithy is still there, but his cycle is much more modern in appearance. Over a period of time, realignments and modifications to roads are easily forgotten. The approach to the bridge was almost straight prior to the building of the new bridge, as can be seen on this reproduction of a postcard.

This remarkable picture must date from around 1870. It is inscribed on the reverse as being taken by J. B. Penfold, Photographer and Painter, of Front Street, Brampton. It shows the more southerly arch of the bridge, with the Bridge Inn in the background. The gable ends of the smithy and the adjoining buildings can be seen to the right of the inn.

The bridge itself is a graceful two-arched structure. Despite the stone plaque set into the wall, which claims that it was built in the second year of the reign of King James II, (1686) it is believed that it was built about 1724, by four local masons, Isaac Monkhouse, of Castle Sowerby, William Railton, of Raughton Head, Philip Simpson, of Sebergham and Joseph Simpson, of Dalston, at a cost of £493. It replaced earlier bridges on the same site, which had either fallen into disrepair or had been swept away by floods.

Lanercost Bridge End Hotel, about 1947

This photograph is taken from the bridge itself, from the refuge built out above the cutwater. I would estimate that it was taken just after World War Two. Apart from the location written on the reverse, there are no other clues to its age.

The old bridge was replaced by the new in 1962 and was completely refurbished in 1998 by the County Council, aided by English Heritage and the National Lottery. A plaque, which records the facts stated above, has been placed on the southern approach.

After the new bridge was opened, it was still possible, for a short time, to drive across the old bridge, but the building of pillars in the carriageway has closed it to vehicular traffic, although pedestrians and cyclists can still use it

The old and new bridges

That the bridge is not safe for traction engines is recorded in tablets of stone! This plaque is on the southern approach to the bridge and, to judge from the heavily lichened appearance, it has been there for a very long time. Perhaps it was the narrowness of the carriageway that made it dangerous – certainly, many of the heavier machines would find it difficult to negotiate.

NAWORTH

There are many more people than I who are better qualified to tell of Naworth and its history. For that reason, I have included pictures with only a little commentary.

This first illustration is a picture postcard view of the castle, probably taken about 1947. It was one of a series of photographic high-quality cards of the town and surrounding area that were sold immediately after the war by Howe's of Brampton. This shows the south front, the view that is perhaps the most familiar to many people. The circular area in the left foreground is the bowling green. There is some evidence that the bowling green was, at one time, converted into a pond. At the time of writing, it is a grassy depression on the left side of the entrance drive.

At the rear of the castle can be seen the short-lived Stanley wing, built in 1894, during the last years of Queen Victoria's reign by Ferguson. This was taken down about 1963.

The next few pictures were copied from the Naworth archives by kind permission of Philip Howard, for whose help and co-operation I am grateful.

It is uncertain who the two croquet players are - probably the girl on the right is Dorothy, who became Lady Henley, with Lady Cecilia.

This is a familiar view of the Castle courtyard, showing the alterations that were made in the 1860s by the 7th Earl, George William Frederick Howard. This adjoining photograph was taken about 1860. He was well-educated, having graduated from Christ Church, Oxford with an M. A.

George William Frederick Howard,
7th Earl of Carlisle, 1802 - 1864.

Degree in 1827. His father died in 1825, whereupon he became known as Lord Morpeth, a courtesy title. He was chosen by his uncle William, the 6th Duke of Devonshire, to accompany him to St. Petersburg to attend the coronation of Tsar Nicholas in 1826. In 1830, he was returned as the Member of Parliament for Yorkshire, topping the poll and he was re-elected at the General Election of 1831, continuing to represent his constituency until 1841. In 1835, Lord Melbourne appointed him to be Chief Secretary for Ireland and later in the year, on May 20th, he was elected to the Privy Council. He proved to be an excellent choice for the position, carrying through several parliamentary bills relating to Ireland, whilst showing that he could more than hold his own in the cut and thrust of debate. His tact was exemplary towards the Irish party and he was admitted to Cabinet rank in 1839. However, in 1841, he lost his seat and resigned his office. There was a set-back in 1842, when he was defeated in a by-election in Dublin, but he returned to the House in 1846 and in June of that year, when Peel's administration fell, was returned once more for the West Riding constituency, being appointed as Commissioner for Woods and Forests in Russell's cabinet. The following year, he was sworn in as Lord Lieutenant of the East Riding. On the death of his father, he became the 7th Earl and took his seat in the House of Lords in 1849. In 1850, he became Chancellor of the Duchy of Lancaster, but when Lord Derby took power in 1852, Lord Carlisle once more resigned his post. 1855 saw him appointed to the Order of the Garter and, in that February, he was appointed as Lord Lieutenant of Ireland, a position he held for three years, resuming the post again in 1859 under Palmerston. He held it until October 1864, when ill health compelled his resignation. He died at Castle Howard in December 1864. We are told that he was an able and kind-hearted man, with cultivated taste and fluency of speech. His gentleness endeared him to all with whom he came into contact. He is the "Man on the Moat", whose statue is now regrettably almost obscured by trees. He never married and was succeeded by his brother, Rev. William George Howard.

George and Rosalind at Naworth in the 1880s. At this time they were merely Mr. and Mrs. Howard.

The 9th Earl was George James, (1843-1911). He was the son of Charles Wentworth George Howard, another brother of the 7th Earl. George married Rosalind Frances Stanley, the daughter of the 2nd Baron Stanley of Alderley, Cheshire, in 1864. The 8th Earl was incapable, so the estates were run by trustees. George and Rosalind, as heirs presumptive, were allowed use of Naworth. She became a champion of the temperance movement and was responsible for the rationalisation of the tremendous number of alehouses in the Brampton area. It is easy to deride Rosalind for her views, but there is no doubt that they were sincerely held. That there was much sadness in her life is indisputable. Of her six sons, five predeceased her, some under tragic circumstances. Christopher, was the first to die in 1896, of pneumonia; Hubert was killed at Omdurman in the Sudan by what is now described euphemistically as 'friendly fire'; Oliver died in Nigeria in 1908; Charles, Lord Morpeth, died of cancer in 1912 and Michael was killed in France in 1917.

The 9th Earl with his sons. From the bottom up: Charles; Hubert, Oliver, Christopher, Geoffrey and Michael

Standing on the left are Hubert and Cecilia. On the back row: George, the 9th Earl, Geoffrey and Rosalind; Christopher (Kit) is standing against the balustrade on the right; Charles is holding the dog, Dorothy and Aurea are sitting on the bottom step, with Oliver seated behind them. The picture probably dates from the early 1890s.

Charles with his children, George, Constance and Ankaret

Charles (1867-1912) was the second child of George and Rosalind – the oldest was Mary Henrietta. Charles married Rhoda Ankaret L'Estrange. His relationship with his mother was not an easy one, as his bride was the daughter of a strongly Tory (Conservative) family. He held the courtesy title of Lord Morpeth and became the 10th Earl on the death of his father in 1911. However, he survived only a short time. He had four children namely: George Josslyn L'Estrange, Constance, Ankaret and Elizabeth. On Charles' death, George became the 11th Earl.

This picture is rather a mystery. It was the occasion of the wedding of Lady Cecilia Howard to Henry Charles Roberts. Are they bridesmaids? If they were, there are almost 130 of them! Certainly, they are all immaculately dressed, beautifully groomed and 'on their best behaviour'.

The Great Hall in the 1890s.

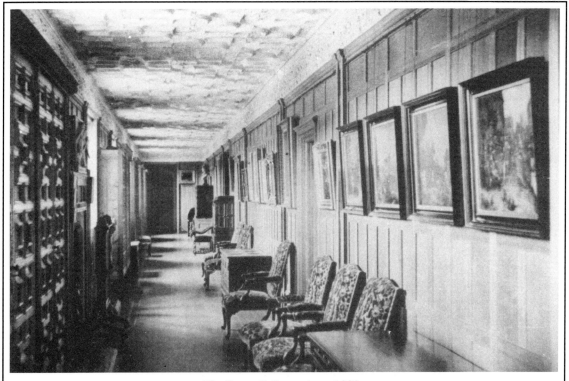

The Long Gallery, about 1890.

The Man on the Moat

THOMAS EDMUNDSON – A RAILWAY PIONEER

Thomas Edmundson was born about 1792 to a Quaker family in Lancaster, an inquisitive and able child, to the extent that his mother taught him to knit to keep him from mischief. At least, she hoped, he would be both useful and quiet! That he had an inventive frame of mind was shown early in his life, when he contrived to connect the baby's crib to the butter churn, ensuring that whenever the churn was in use, the child would be lulled to sleep. He was apprenticed as a cabinetmaker, later going into partnership in a business in Carlisle. This failed, however and he was bankrupted. Nevertheless, that training would be put to great practical use in later days.

Brampton station in the 1970s, before its demolition.

It was for the reason that he needed work that he joined the newly built Newcastle and Carlisle Railway at a salary of £60 per year, serving at Milton, as the present Brampton station was then known. There is some dispute as to his position there – some have him as a booking clerk and others as the stationmaster. Whichever it was, he was soon well acquainted with the miseries of the railway's booking system. It was very complicated in operation and equally time-consuming in its implementation. The details of the tickets, including the passengers' names, had to be entered into a ledger and the tickets written out by hand. At smaller stations, the passengers paid their fare to the stationmaster, who then issued the ticket before passing the money to the guard. Probably Milton worked this aspect of the railway's regulations.

His incredible vision was that this process could be mechanised. Within a year, he had devised his own method of hand printing tickets cut from cardboard. Just another year later, he had developed a machine that printed the tickets, whilst an automatic counting device numbered the tickets as they came from the press. The whole system, he recounted later, came to him in one single flash of inspiration.

This operation took place initially only at Milton, but was extended to other stations. Promotion was in the offing for Thomas – the railway proposed to move him to Newcastle. However, in 1839, Captain Laws of the Manchester and Leeds Railway offered him a doubling of his salary if he would work for his company. Thomas naturally accepted! Later, he opened a factory in Manchester to produce ticket blanks, machines, presses and racks to meet the constantly increasing demands put upon him. In just a few years, the Edmundson ticketing system was in use, not only all over this country, but also worldwide. It was so simple and effective that it wasn't bettered until computers came into use. Only a few years ago, I was issued with an Edmundson-style ticket in Germany, date stamped in the old familiar method with that familiar 'double thump' that many might remember from bygone days. Because of his genius, a man who should only have made an insignificant mark on history became a famous name in railway business. Thomas did well from his invention. He patented it and charged a royalty of ten shillings per mile per annum, that is to say, any company using the system paid him that sum for every mile they owned. If they had three hundred miles of track, he received £150 each year from them. According to records of his life, 'he worked out his invention with skill and patience, enjoyed its honours with modesty and dispensed its fruits with generosity.'

This assortment of tickets, all using the Edmundson system, are mainly from Britain, but there are three from Germany, one from Eire and one from Romania included. The ticket size is constant throughout the different railways, 2¼" x 1 3/16" (57mm by 30 mm) and the method of dating, as shown on the middle ticket on the bottom row, is also uniform. It will be noted that even in the 1960s, when the Burnley to Mill Hill ticket was issued, some tickets still had to be handwritten – both the journeys illustrated were only about twelve miles, but yet there were no tickets ready printed to cover them!

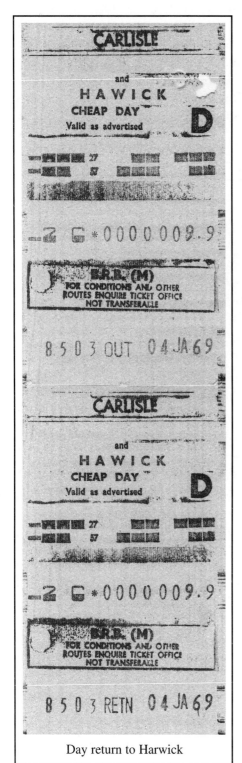

Day return to Harwick

What a tragedy it was when the Brampton Junction station buildings were demolished! A part of our railway heritage was destroyed by that wanton destruction. It could have provided a monument and a museum to a man whose vision revolutionised the simple act of issuing a railway ticket.

The computerised system that superseded the simple Edmundson card ticket produced some huge sheets of paper. Even allowing for the fact that everything was done to simplify the accounting, the result was an unwieldy and fragile article. The printing was frequently almost illegible and there was a tremendous amount of wasted space. This example shown was purchased on the last day of operation of the Waverley Line from Carlisle to Edinburgh.

Matters have improved now, as the tickets are now 'credit card' sized, but they are still almost three times larger and carry no more information that they did when Thomas's stroke of genius conceived the idea over a century and a half ago!

This little cartouche is an engraving of a train on the Newcastle to Carlisle Railway. Their running practice was different from the regulation that applies today, in that trains ran on the right hand track.

METHODIST CHURCHES OF BRAMPTON

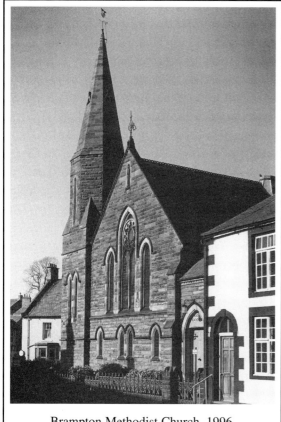

Brampton Methodist Church, 1996.

This familiar building at the head of Main Street is the Church that was built by the Wesleyan Methodists just over a hundred years ago. It is seen here from the eastern side in 1996. The white building seen on the left is 'Oval House', one of the oldest buildings in the town.

The first Methodist Church in the town can be traced back with certainty to 1807, but it is known that the cause has long been in the town. There was a society worshipping here in 1789, a fact that is recorded in Hutchinson's 'History of Cumberland'. The location was possibly a meetinghouse in the yard of the 'Scotch Arms' Hotel. This was still during John Wesley's lifetime, the founder of Methodism, who paid several visits to the area. However, the history of the local movement might go even further back, as there was a preacher by the name of William Linnell living in the town. It would appear most unlikely that Linnell would not have conducted meetings in the locality. Although his story was described in the previous book about the town, he is a part of the story of Methodism in the town, so I crave indulgence for mentioning him again.

William Linnell was a native of the village of Whittlesbury, Northamptonshire and was first appointed by the Methodist Conference, about 1770, to serve in Cheshire. From there, he came north to Whitehaven and finally to Brampton, where it is recorded in the minutes of the Conference that, 'he has ceased to travel'. Obviously, he had put down roots and was unwilling to move to a new appointment as was, and still is, the custom of the Methodist Church. Certainly, he had married a young woman from Brampton, Eleanor Blenkinsop, whilst he was still at St. Bees in June 1773, making his home in Craw Hall. He died in February, 1779, aged 36 and was interred in the Old Church graveyard, where his restored gravestone may still be seen. It is said that Charles Wesley, the great Methodist hymnwriter, wrote his epitaph, but this is hard to accept, as the verse is poor doggerel.

William Linnell's grave in the Old Church yard.

The remnant of the oldest exclusively Methodist Church can still be seen in Chapel Lane, on the north side of Main Street. It is possible that this building was actually opened in 1799 and the sum of £140 that was mentioned in 1807 for its construction could, in fact, be for its alteration and enlargement. In 1817, it was again enlarged by the addition of galleries at a cost of £120. This relatively large expenditure must have required a great act of faith by the Trustees, the same leap that the present members are facing in 2002 for the replacement of the Church Hall and redevelopment at the rear of the Church.

Bethesda Chapel on Main Street, 2002.

Methodism splintered into various groups about the turn of the nineteenth century. One of the larger groups was the Primitive Methodists. They erected a church in Back Street (now Main Street) in 1823, following a visit from one of Primitive Methodism's great preachers, William Clowes. William Wheelan's book, 'The History and Topography of Cumberland' makes mention that he preached in the open air to large audiences on several occasions and these large gatherings were instrumental in providing the incentive to build a new place of worship. This neat little building, Bethesda Chapel, at the end of the row of cottages in Main Street, stands across the road from Hadrian's statue and is presently used by The Brethren, an evangelical church.

In 1836, the Wesleyan Methodists built a new Chapel at the bottom of Gelt Road. This was a large two-storey building, which could accommodate about 600 people, a figure which would represent about a quarter of Brampton's population at that time! However, it was deemed to be too large, so it was divided to make the upper portion the church and the lower was used as the Sunday School. Much later, the upper storey was removed and the building was used by Howe of Brampton as their print works. Later still, it took on its present guise as A.B.W. Hardware. To the practised eye, even in its truncated form, it still shows its origin as a Methodist Chapel.

The 'Carlisle Patriot' provided a graphic report of the opening:

"On Sunday last, a very neat and commodious Wesleyan Chapel, capable of seating 600 persons, was opened for public worship at Brampton. The Rev. James Everitt of Newcastle-upon-Tyne preached in the forenoon and evening and the Rev. Percy Strutt in the afternoon. On the following Tuesday, Mr. W. Dawson, of Barnbow near Leeds, preached in the afternoon and evening. A very respectable party, amounting to 500 persons, took tea in the Assembly Room of the Howard Arms, which was tastefully decorated for the occasion. A number of ladies gratuitously furnished the provisions needed and the proceeds of the tickets sold were given to the Trust Funds. After tea, the company was addressed by Messrs. Dawson, Moorhouse Wild, Stokoe and Atkinson. The collections at the opening amounted to £46 and the proceeds of the meeting to £26, a total of £72."

The former Wesleyan Methodist Chapel at the foot of Gelt Road, 2002.

Such a gathering and a collection of that size would appear to indicate a very active community of Methodism in Brampton, forming a strong and flourishing society. In April,1878, the Trustees of the Primitive Methodists held a meeting to propose construction of a new Chapel. The result was the erection of the Moat Side building, which opened in 1879. This still stands today and, with some alteration, is in use as the Brampton Playhouse.

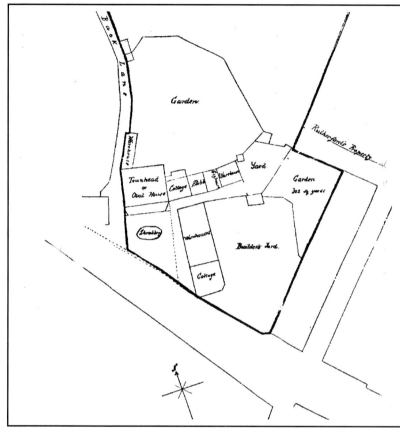

In March 1898, the Quarterly Meeting of the Wesleyan Trustees accepted a motion that a new Chapel be erected at the eastern end of Main Street. The agreement to purchase the site, which had previously been Messrs. Routledge's builders' yard, shown on the accompanying plan, was drawn up on May 10th, 1899. The site was cleared and prepared for the laying of the foundation stones in July of the same year.

The collection of gifts and donations amounted to £712. By November 1900, the congregation had moved to the new building, the present Methodist church. Again, the newspapers of the following day, November 8th, gave a detailed description of the proceedings, under the headline, 'Opening of the New Wesleyan Church at Brampton'.

The laying of the foundation stone of the new Wesley Chapel, July 1899.

"*Yesterday afternoon, the new Wesleyan Church at Brampton, the foundation stones of which were laid on July 6th last year, was opened for worship by Rev. Thomas Waugh, the well-known evangelist, whose parents live at Middle Farm, Brampton. "It may be briefly stated here that a meeting of the Trustees held upwards of two years ago found that to put the old chapel in proper repair and alter it in accordance with modern requirements would cost about £1300. The trustees thereupon decided to build a new church. One of the prime movers of the scheme was*

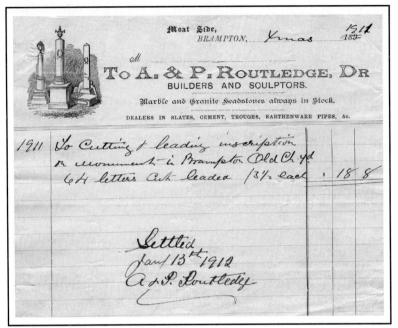

the Rev. Thomas Waugh, who entered with such zeal into the work that he was able, when the foundation stones were laid, to pay over to the Trustees the sum of £442, which he himself has collected from his friends. Since then, he has collected another £80.

The Trustees obtained a site in Moat Side at a cost of £650. The style of the architecture is Early Gothic: the red sandstone of Gelt has been used for the body of the building, with white stone for the doors and windows. The effect is eminently churchlike and the interior arrangements are as perfect as skill and experience could suggest. There is accommodation for 400 worshippers.

The architect was Mr. John Wills of Derby and London and the contactors were:- Mason work: Mr. T. Telfer of Langholm; Joinery work: Mr. J. H. Reed, Carlisle; Plastering: Mr. W. Barker, Brampton; Painting and glazing: Messrs. Penfold and Son, Brampton; Plumbing: Messrs. Wallace and Allen, Glasgow; Heating: Mr. Corbett of Carlisle. The cost of the building, including the architect's fees, but exclusive of the cost of the land, will be about £2350. The opening ceremony was fixed for three o'clock and shortly before that hour, the Rev. Thomas Waugh presented himself at the main entrance and, having given the customary knocks, the door was opened and the building crammed to excess by an influential congregation, great numbers having travelled considerable distances. The Rev. F. N. Naylor (Minister) notified that the building had been registered as a place for public worship and solemnisation of marriages. Special hymns were sung, Mr. John Armstrong presiding at the organ. The service was conducted by Rev. T. Waugh, who also preached the sermon from the text 'He is head of the body, the church'. The discourse was a very practical one, delivered with all the powers and lucidity for which the preacher had obtained a reputation.

A public tea was subsequently held in the Tweed Mill, presided over by a large number of ladies, there being a very big attendance. At six o'clock, a largely attended meeting was held in the New Hall of the Tweed Mill, kindly lent by Lady Carlisle, which was presided over by Mr. T. H. Bainbridge, J.P. of Newcastle and addresses were given by Rev T. Waugh, Rev F. Naylor, Mr. E. Westmorland of Carlisle and others.

Other changes were the provision of a new organ in 1910. To mark its inception, a recital was given by Mr. Charles Bowes of Newcastle. In the mid 1980s, some pews were removed from the rear of the church to create a larger and roomier circulating area. One other significant change, as a result, was the provision of an 'Upper Room', which has proved invaluable for group meetings, as well as providing an overspill gallery for those occasions when the church is filled to overflowing, such as the popular Town Carol Service.

In 1994, a new vestry, which was built in matching stone, was added to the side and rear of the church. This addition has created a much-needed improvement, as the old vestry was dark, dismal and cramped. It was consecrated by Rev. Bryan Hoare, who was then president of the Methodist Conference.

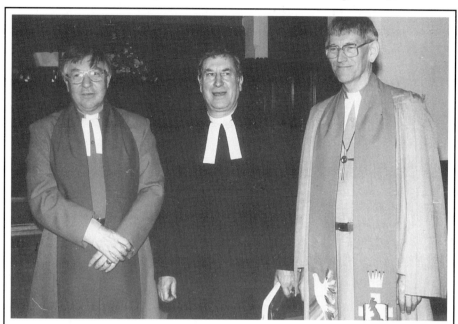

The occasion of the dedication of the new vestry of the Methodist Church on April 14th, 1994. From right to left are Revd. Donald Frith, who was the Chairman of the Cumbria District and is now Superintendent Minister of the Brampton Circuit, Rev. Ronald Morris, the then Minister of Brampton and Rev. Bryan Hoare, Chairman of the Methodist Conference

What of the future? A new church hall is proposed, to replace the old one, which is now a hundred years old and in desperate need of renovation. As with the forefathers, demolition and rebuilding will be the order of the day, the sole difference being that of cost!

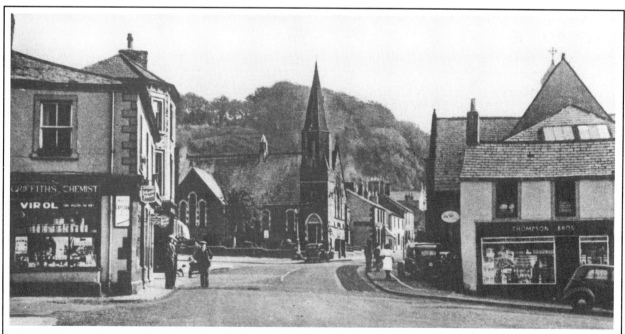

The Methodist Church is in the centre of this picture. We are looking east from the top of High Cross Street in the late 1940s. Griffiths' chemist's shop is now Butterworth's solicitors' office, Thompson's grocer's has become Kyle's butcher's. There have been changes in the layout of the top of High Cross Street, as there are now car parking bays there. The general appearance, however, is not much changed.

MAIN STREET

This picture, taken during the 1937 Coronation celebrations, is interesting because it shows two features that have gone from the Brampton scene. On the right of the picture can be seen a cottage doorway, immediately alongside the shop of Atkinson and Sons, who were long-established decorators in the town. The cottage was demolished many years ago, but its position can still be recognised by the small buttress that is now part of the shop wall.

The second picture was taken in February, 2000 and shows that the decorator's has now become a Pizza shop. The fence in the background hides the site of what was once a stone building used as a garage. It is sometimes asked why the low stone wall cannot be removed from the lower end of Union Lane to make less of a bottleneck - it prevents large vehicles using it as a short cut to and from Longtown Road.

Bottom of Union Lane, February 2000

In the early years of this century, the decorator's business was owned by Ephraim Steel.

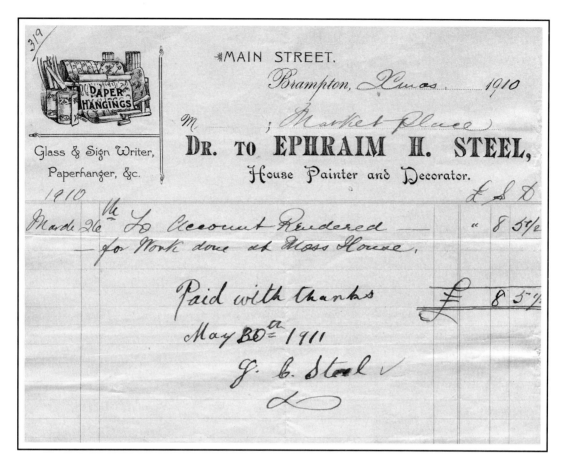

Isaac Hodgson's printing works occupied those premises that are now Mitchelson's newsagent's shop. Later, the business was taken over by Harding and Irving's. Between them, the two firms published a wealth of brochures, maps, guide books and postcards of the town and the surrounding area.

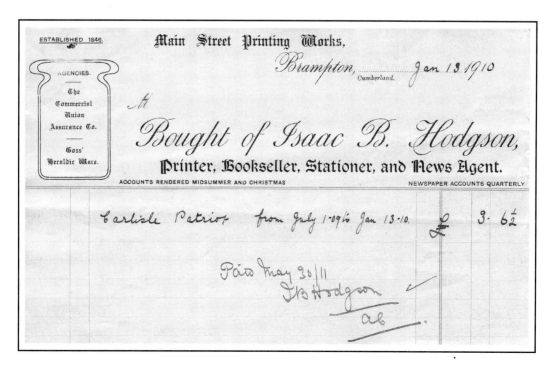

The building that is now known as 'Laurel House' was formerly the Liberal Club. In this 1931 picture, repairs are being done to the leading on the roof. The workers are Percy Campbell, his son and Tom Armstrong. It was bought by the Brampton Old People's Welfare Committee about 1960, after the Liberal Club decided to close. This committee had first met in April, 1959 and invitations were issued to all organisations interested or connected with the welfare of the elderly. After their third meeting, the building was offered for sale at a much-reduced price to the committee and they decided, after consultations, to purchase and modify this suitable building in an excellent position in the town. It is stated that the committee didn't have a penny to its name – the whole venture was an act of great faith! Once the decision had been made, an appeal was sent to the town for funds and there was a wonderful response. The initial debt of £2400 was reduced, in less than a year, to £550.

Many services were offered, such as health visiting and chiropody. There was a great deal of help forthcoming to bring the club into being. Members themselves scrubbed out and painted after alterations had been completed. Cheap paint was acquired and the decorators' businesses of the town helped, as did boys from Edmond Castle School.

The Club was opened in April 1961 by Tim Westoll, then Chairman of Cumberland County Council. Fundraising was still necessary to pay off the remainder of the debt and to settle accounts for coal, electricity and other repairs. The Brampton Old People's Association, which had been formed just after the Queen's coronation in June 1953, agreed to support the venture by using the building for their functions. One ambitious project was the provision of hot meals for those living alone who did not cook for themselves. A rota was formed and this has proved to be a very welcome benefit. It still provides a valued meeting place for the more senior citizens of the town.

On the right of the Liberal Club was Claude Shipley's garage and cycle repair shop. One childhood memory is of petrol tins, an essential if one were setting out on a journey of any length, with Pratt's name embossed on them. Their logotype appears on the petrol pump seen in front of the garage.

It hasn't been possible to establish exactly where James Hewitt's cycle shop was located. The mention of Shipley's seems as good a place as any to show a copy of his account, as Shipley's also attended to bicycle repairs.

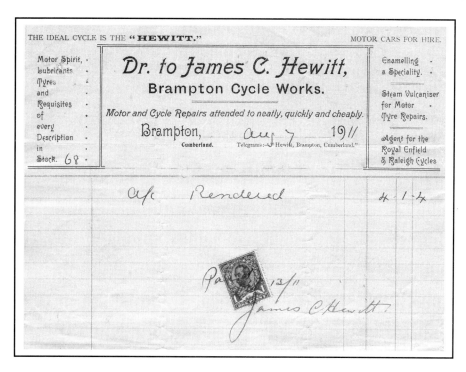

'Laurel House', 1997

The second photograph was taken after the opening of the bypass, as can be seen by the road sign on the pavement. This shows Main Street has changed from being a trunk road, the A69 and has become the A6071, a number previously restricted to the Brampton – Longtown – Gretna road. The trunk road's number now appears in brackets, indicating that the road to Carlisle can be reached by travelling in that direction. Note the parking bay in front of Laurel House – this follows the old pavement line from the time when the central block stood in the middle of High Cross Street. It remains on the same line, over seventy years after the demolition. The garage has become an antique shop.

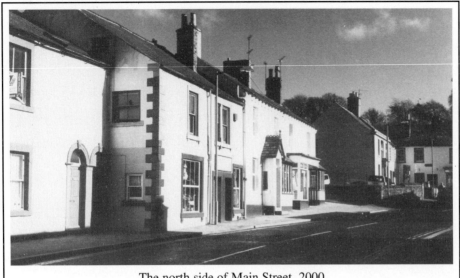

The north side of Main Street, 2000

This is a modern picture of the north side of Main Street opposite the Central Place car park. This parking area was created after the clearance of sub-standard housing in Central Place and Cow Lane during the 1950s. The building seen in the far distance was for many years a pharmacy and is now a solicitor and estate agent's office.

Next comes 'Laurel House', then Falkins Hill, with car parking space at its foot. For many years, other buildings stood here. At the bottom of the hill stood Dixon's, a game and fish merchant's, then came Smith's, the 'Cheap Shop', shown in the picture dating from about 1900. This was taken over to become Samuel Hetherington's boot and shoe shop. Although this picture has been used in a previous book, I have included it once more to show the building as it appears in the picture of Main Street of 1898.

The shop with the bay window is Elliott's decorator's. It was previously the 'Wheatsheaf Inn', which was run by Henry Gleed in 1901. This fell victim to Lady Carlisle's vigorous temperance campaign in the early years of the last century, the effects of which were discussed in 'The Changing Face of Brampton', which included a list of the former taverns and alehouses, which, in its turn, was derived from a talk given by Peter Burn in 1896.

Smith's, the Cheap Shop', about 1898

This earlier illustration shows, at the end of Chapel Lane, the building already mentioned that was occupied by Hetherington's. This building was situated on the east side of the lane, across from the little cottage whose end wall is shown in the illustration. Chapel Lane itself has been marked by one

of the new street nameplates fixed last year.

These new signs are barely distinguishable from the older ones of 1894, which provoked such an outcry about the cost (9d. per letter!) when the parish council decided on their provision. The Beck Lane sign is an original.

From the children's style of dress in the lower picture, it would appear to be about 1900. The more recent top picture shows that Hetherington's has vanished, to be replaced by the much smaller block of public conveniences. These, too, are now part of history, having been replaced by a newer building in Central Place.

Westward down the street is White House, which was owned by the Carrick family, then the Lees in the nineteenth century. The two photographs shown here, copied from postcards, are not very different, one from the other. The trees have changed, but it is what can be seen in the distance that has altered greatly.

Main Street, pre-war – the railings are still on the wall of White House.

Main Street, about 1900

Some photographs of the interior of the 'White House', taken in 1893, have come to light. The entrance hall will be familiar to many generations of Grammar School pupils who passed through it in the course of their schooldays. The beautifully panelled ceiling is still in place after the sensitive conversion of the building into two homes.

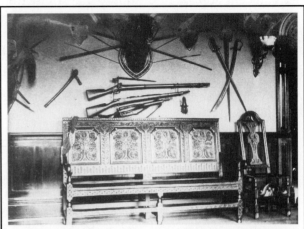

White house as renovated in 1999

About 1894, a circus must have visited the town. A series of pictures, unfortunately not of the highest quality as were many photographs at that time, were taken of the procession through the town.

The man with four horses is directly aligned with the entry to the Scotch Arms' Mews archway. Cairns' shop shows that he was a watchmaker, but his name does not appear in the 1901 Directory of the town. The shop to the right of the archway is that of William Routledge.

He was the proprietor of the 'Scotch Arms' at some time in the 1890s. There is an entry for him in that Directory, but not as a purveyor of wines, spirits and tobacco, as appears on the shop front. That shop front is clearer, but not much, on the picture with the elephants and camels.

In the third picture, the camels have passed and we are looking west towards the corner of what was known unofficially as Edger's Lane – the cabinetmaker's is the double-fronted shop behind the man riding the elephant. In the final picture, there is an uninterrupted view along the street, now

36

empty of animals, save for what seems to be a solitary donkey and a white blob, which might be a goose.

Edger's Lane is that short length of 'street' that gives pedestrian access to the recently improved and rebuilt property behind Main Street. William Edger was a man of many talents. In addition to his woodworking skills, he also took a great interest in the Silver band.

On the bend of Main Street is 'The Hollies'. This fine Georgian House was threatened with demolition in the not-too-distant past. This picture shows it in 1976.

The roof of 'The Hollies' can be seen in the foreground of the next photograph, which dates from 1893. Behind it lies Carrick's Yard. The White House is on the extreme right of the picture, with the cottages of Bank Court in front of it. Had one been so minded, during the summer of 1904, it would have been possible to have rented 'White House' for a stay, an early example of a 'holiday let'.

'The Hollies' in 1976

TO BE LET
For the Summer Months.

Delightful Summer Residence at Brampton, Cumberland.

TO BE LET FURNISHED during the whole or any part of the months of JUNE, JULY, AUGUST, SEPTEMBER, AND OCTOBER, a large and beautifully situated MANSION HOUSE AND GROUNDS, AT BRAMPTON, CUMBERLAND. The House comprises, 5 Reception and Sitting Rooms, 8 Bedrooms, large and convenient Kitchens, Pantries, and all the usual offices and conveniences of a modern Country Gentleman's Residence. STABLING for 4 horses with Brougham, Dog Cart and Spring Cart if desired.

The Grounds are beautifully laid out and the produce of the Kitchen Gardens and Orchards can be had by arrangement. TENNIS AND CROQUET LAWNS. Close to the Town, Railway, and Post Office. Boating and Fishing within 1½ miles.

The House is situate near the Town of Brampton in one of the most beautiful parts of the County of Cumberland within 2 miles of Naworth Castle, the Border seat of the Earl of Carlisle ; Lanercost Abbey, the beautiful Gelt Woods, and the Lake known as Talkin Tarn, where fishing and excellent boating can be had. It is also within easy distance of Gilsland, a well known watering place ; the famous Corby Castle Woods, the Nunnery Walks, and the Roman Wall. The rivers of Eden, Irthing and Gelt are all in close proximity and provide the very best Salmon and Trout Fishing. The Cumberland Lake District is also easily reached from Brampton.

For further particulars apply to

CARRICK, LEE, & SONS,
Solicitors,
Brampton, Cumberland.

The veiw north-east from St.Martin's church tower in 1893. The large building is the Workhouse.

In the distance is the Brampton Union Workhouse. This is the only picture that I have seen which shows this building. They were a source of dread to the aged and infirm in bygone days because of the strict regimes practiced within the walls. However, it was not only the elderly who had cause to fear. Other unfortunates were among the inmates committed into its care: young women who produced children out of wedlock and were turned out by their families could be interned there. 'Travellers' were expected to work to pay for their night's shelter.

This was the scene at the bottom of Longtown Road during the major flood in the summer of 1982. The town was very effectively severed by the floodwater as the beck overflowed, inundating all the streets along its course and causing a great deal of damage.

Longtown Road, from behind the Police Station, 1982

It is not known who is the driver of this venerable machine, or even who owned it. It might, perhaps, belong to the owner of the New Brewery, which is where the picture was taken. One can only wonder at the toughness of the old motorists!

The car is a Daimler tonneau of about 1902 or 1903 vintage and is either a 16 or 22 hp model. It was the first of the name to carry the characteristic 'fluting' on the radiator, which makes the Daimler marque instantly recognisable even today. This car was designed by the American-born Percy Martin. In 1906, the manufacturers altered the position of the flutes from the sides to the top of the radiator. (I am indebted for this information to 'Honest John' of the *'Daily Telegraph'*.)

The term 'New Brewery' is relative – it was opened in 1790, in contrast to the Old Brewery, which was opened in 1785! It is now a tastefully converted private house.

Bert Pugh

The Brampton gasworks stood behind the cottages on Carlisle Road. In the 1970s, when North Sea gas came to the town, the works closed. They were quickly demolished and all traces disappeared. The site is now used for car parking. Although tantalising glimpses of the complex can be seen on some old pictures and postcards, no photographs had ever materialised until March this year. Two pictures show the gasholder, with Bert Pugh in the first and Harry Preston in the second. The third, the oxide boxes, were used as a filter of some kind for removal of impurities. The children are, from left to right, Minnie Pugh and her brother Ernie, with their cousin, Maureen Pugh.

During the last war, the two men responsible for the gasworks both joined the Home Guard. Because it was essential for one or other to be there at any time 'just in case', the roll call always featured the unusual name 'Smith-or-Pugh', depending on who was free for Home Guard duty that evening!

Harry Preston

BRAMPTON GAS COMPANY.

BRAMPTON, *May 6 1911*

M *Bank House*

To Brampton Gas Light & Coke Co., Dr.

Index.	Gas consumed in 100 cubic feet.	Price per 1000 feet.	Amount		
Present half-year 299	21000	3/9	3	18	9
Last half-year 089				1	6
Rent of Meter					
			4	0	3

Accounts are due on June 21st and December 21st. It is requested that payment of this account be paid to the Secretary when it is rendered.

This picture is taken on the old allotments, which lay on the south side of the main road, to the rear of St. Martin's. The site is now covered by 'Jerusalem'. The young girl is Alma Findlay (now Forster) and her grandfather, Bert Pugh.

In the background can be seen the junction of Main Street and Longtown Road – the white building on the extreme right is 'Garden Hill' House and the house with the large chimney stack protruding from halfway up the roof and with the whitened window surrounds is the house, which was previously the shop at 2, Longtown Road. St. Martin's Terrace is partially hidden by the fir tree just behind the gate.

Osborne's was a shop on Main Street, but I have not managed to discover its exact whereabouts. Readers might have noticed the long-obsolete practice to be seen on these old accounts, that of signing the receipt over a stamp if the amount was more than two pounds.

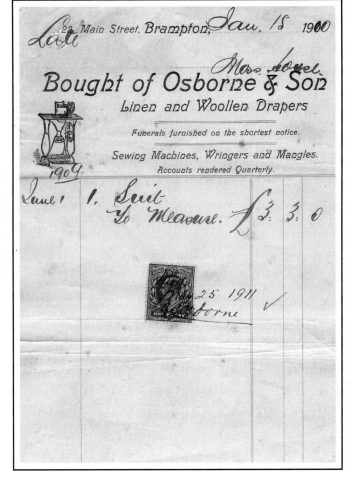

At the lower end of Main Street was Kindred's blacksmith's shop. This was wound up around 1945 and the whole of the equipment was sold by the Farmers' Mart at Longtown.

Later, there was some disagreement with the District Valuer of the Inland Revenue about the value of the site, as detailed in the letter below.

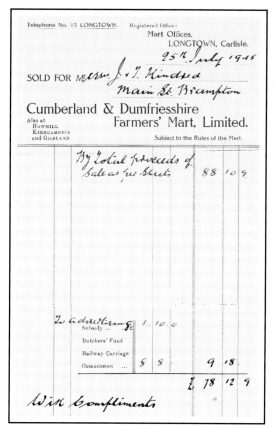

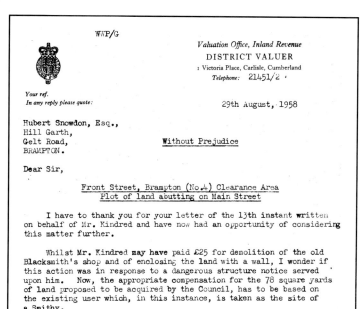

Valuation Office, Inland Revenue
DISTRICT VALUER
1 Victoria Place, Carlisle, Cumberland
Telephone: 21451/2

Your ref.
In any reply please quote:

29th August, 1958

Hubert Snowdon, Esq.,
Hill Garth,
Gelt Road,
BRAMPTON.

Without Prejudice

Dear Sir,

Front Street, Brampton (No.4) Clearance Area
Plot of land abutting on Main Street

I have to thank you for your letter of the 13th instant written on behalf of Mr. Kindred and have now had an opportunity of considering this matter further.

Whilst Mr. Kindred may have paid £25 for demolition of the old Blacksmith's shop and of enclosing the land with a wall, I wonder if this action was in response to a dangerous structure notice served upon him. Now, the appropriate compensation for the 78 square yards of land proposed to be acquired by the Council, has to be based on the existing user which, in this instance, is taken as the site of a Smithy.

Having regard to the smallness of the site and the difficulty of getting plans passed for any new building to be erected thereon, I imagine that it is hardly saleable. In fact, Mr. Kindred may have been endeavouring to sell it for some time without success.

You ask me to put forward an offer for the land and consequently, having given careful consideration to the matter, I think that £15 would be the appropriate figure for the Council to pay. They would also, of course, pay the proper legal costs of Mr. Kindred in connection with the conveyance of the land. Perhaps you will let me know if Mr. Kindred is prepared to accept this sum and at the same time state the name of the Solicitor who will act for him in this matter.

Yours faithfully,

District Valuer.

It is hard to believe that a plot of land in the town could be sold for just £15! However, this does work out at about £930 per acre, a considerable sum of money in those days. The lower picture shows the dereliction of the lower end of Main Street before the demolition of the properties.

The site of Kindred's yard, taken about 1957.

CLEANING THE STREETS

It is said that, in the middle of the nineteenth century, the Brampton Back Street, now known as Main Street, was one of the filthiest streets in Cumberland. Something had to be done about this state of affairs. The body responsible, strange though it may appear in this day and age, when the District Council or the Parish Council hold such accountability, was the Parish Church Vestry. At that time, they could levy a rate on the parish. Some twenty years ago, a fascinating public notice came to light, preserved amongst the various papers at the Parish Church, which shows just how it was done.

To the Ratepayers of Brampton
NOTICE OF RESOLUTIONS
to be proposed at a Vestry Meeting, to be held in the
VESTRY ROOM
of Brampton Parish Church on an early day, due
notice of which will be given by the Churchwardens
and Overseers, viz:-

That a rate of 6d ($2^1/_2$p) in the Pound on the Poor Rate Assessment be levied for all or some of the following Purposes, viz:-

For repairing and amending the Pavement from the Swartle, over Pickering's Hill, along the Back Street, through Low Cross Street, Cow Lane, Souter Holme Alley and elsewhere:

For adjusting the Levels of Gutters and Channel Gradients, to effect a complete Surface Drainage and outfall:

For cutting, with the consent of the Lord of the Manor, a site, 30 ft. by 15 ft., in the Lonning Moat next to the road and another site in the base of the Moat abutting on the Highway, and for erection thereon of two Public Privies with separate compartments for both sexes.

For the purchase of a Scavinger's Cart, Shovel and Spade, or a four-wheeled Truck with a pair of shafts, for Town Uses.

That a Contract be entered into with a fit person or persons jointly, to rake the Streets and Thoroughfares: to collect, remove and take away all deposit therefrom weekly: and half-yearly or oftener to empty all Public and private Privies and Midden Steads and in consideration of the party or parties so contracting to reserve or retain, by way of remuneration and in lieu of part payment, all manner of Street Deposit, Privy and Midden Deposit and other Refuse Soil, and that the Inhabitants be required to scatter or sink Ashes or House Sweepings down their privies, placing washing or other soiled water where the same can flow, otherwise to deliver their Ashes, House Sweepings and other dry refuse to the scavinger weekly.

JAMES BURROUGH, Brampton, 13th. October, 1868
Intending Resident.

The Swartle is the old name for Lanercost Road, Pickering's Hill is Moatside, Cow Lane was the lane running from Main Street to Beck Lane at the White Lion, Souter Holme was part of High Cross Street. The 'Lonning Moat' is a mystery. The Lonning was Gelt Road, but whether the notice refers to this or somewhere in the region of the Moat isn't known.

The privilege offered, of keeping the refuse from privies and horses, seems scant reward for so much hard work! Note the older spelling of 'scavenger'. The printers of the document were Cheesbrough's of Front Street.

PRINTING IN BRAMPTON

Isaac B. Hodgson was responsible for the first established printing work in Brampton in 1842. It was opened over the shop in Main Street that is now Mitchelson's newsagents. He produced many booklets about the town and the surrounding district, along with picture postcards. Many of his publications can still be found – some ideas from them have been used in this book.

He was the uncle of Bertha Hewetson, whose father, Topping Hewetson, was a veterinary surgeon who lived at 'The Hollies' on Main Street. Bertha married Brian Sullivan and lived on Station Road, before having a house built at 'Dandy How', from where they moved to West Cumberland. After the father's death, all of the papers relevant to the business were removed by a Dr. Hewetson, Bertha's brother, who lived in London.

Messrs. Harding and Irving took over the business from Hodgson. Again, this was a very prolific and forward-looking firm, providing the same type of products as had Isaac Hodgson. Richard Howe and Hugh Barnes both worked for the firm. Tom Irving, one of the proprietors, was Hugh's uncle. Mr. Irving asked Richard to take over the business, but he didn't feel that this was right to go above Hugh. Thus, the two men ran the firm from about 1937 until the end of the war in 1945. Upon Hugh's demobilisation from the services in that year, it was decided to split the firm – Hugh took the stationery and Richard the printing side.

Richard Howe's eldest son, Richard Austen Howe, was in printing with his father, but he had been called up for service in the Royal Navy. Another son, Joe, was working at the time at E. W. Cates' motor

119 YEARS OF UNBROKEN SERVICE

PROOF OF STABILITY

The above is the Trade Mark of the Founder, the late Isaac Barnfather Hodgson, who commenced business in the year 1842.

HOWE OF BRAMPTON LTD.
PRINTERS, STATIONERS, CONFECTIONERS AND NEWSAGENTS

GELT PRINTING WORKS
10, 12 and 32 FRONT STREET
Telephone 447

Printed by Howe of Brampton Ltd., Brampton, Cumberland.

engineering and filling station at Low Row. He was asked to join the firm. Soon after, Cheesbrough's, the other printers in the town, ceased trading and Richard took over their premises and all the equipment at Beck Lane. Later, when Howe and Barnes split the business, all the type and machinery was moved into the Beck Lane works, with the exception of the Eagle press, which was an enormous piece of engineering. It was able to print 35" x 22½", known as a 'Double Demi', a sheet size used before metrication. This press was left in the Main Street building, as it was feared that moving it might possibly damage the building's structure! It remained there until Mitchelson's took over the business, when it was dismantled and transported to the Beamish Museum, where it remains in store. It is believed that it was originally used to print the 'Glasgow Herald'.

Cheesbrough's had a newspaper and stationery shop at 28, Front Street, which is now the barber's shop owned by Mark O'Neill. At the back of that shop, there is still a connecting door to be seen, which leads into a passage over the yard and into the print works immediately behind. The family lived "above the shop" at no. 30.

Later, Richard Howe bought premises in Gelt Road, which had previously been the Wesleyan Methodist Chapel. Prior to this acquisition, it had been used by Bob Telford as a joiner's shop. This was burnt out and sold to Jack Pratt. His sons, brothers Jack and Tommy Pratt, used it as a garage and warehouse for two wagons, which transported large bales of wool from Ireland. It was for this reason that the doors were heightened to allow access for the massive loads. During the second world war, the building was requisitioned by the Ministry of Food for the storage of emergency dry goods. The whole business was taken over by Dumfries Newspapers, who moved their operations to the Industrial Estate, where they still traded under the name Howe of Brampton. In the early part of 2001, this works was closed under rationalisation plans and its whole function was transferred to Annan, so bringing to an end almost 170 years of printing in the town.

I am greatly indebted to Joe Howe for checking the information contained in this little chapter.

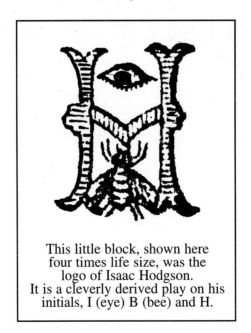

This little block, shown here four times life size, was the logo of Isaac Hodgson. It is a cleverly derived play on his initials, I (eye) B (bee) and H.

There is another connection linked with the town to printing on a much vaster scale, which is discussed in the next section.

GEORGE ROUTLEDGE:
IS THIS MAN BRAMPTON'S GREATEST SON?

George Routledge with his second wife,
Mary Grace Bell

There will probably be very few people in Brampton and district who have heard of George Routledge, who was born in Brampton on September 23rd, 1812. Despite that, he is probably the most successful man who was a native of the town.

He was apprenticed to Charles Thurnam, the Carlisle bookseller, when he was fifteen, but after six years, he asked to be prematurely released from that contract. That achieved, he went, as did so many young men, to London to seek his fortune. He was given employment by a large publishing firm in Paternoster Row and he clearly made a satisfactory impression, as his salary increased over the next three years and he was made head of the binding department. However, the company began to decline, so George decided to branch out on his own account. He acquired a shop in Ryder's Court, near Leicester Square and hired a fifteen-year-old William Henry Warne, whose older sister, Maria Elizabeth, he married within twelve months. It would appear that he could not support a wife merely by bookselling, as he took on a full-time position at the Tithe Office, Somerset House. Young Warne was left in charge at the shop. The move was obviously successful. William managed the business during the day, which left Routledge free to work in the evenings building up his stock and adding other lines of stationery.

He even ventured into print himself and wrote a guidebook called 'The Beauties of Gilsland'. This was a failure, but it taught him the valuable lesson of patience before rushing into the printing of any book. In 1840, he joined with Baldwin, Craddock and Joy, his original employers in London, in a reprint of a novel by Maria Edgworth entitled 'Harry and Lucy', but he soon realised that it was far more rewarding to sell remainders from other firms, rather than sharing in the cost of new works. It was an balancing equation of small profit but quick return – such trade yielded large dividends, a lesson he never forgot. In 1843, he expanded his business by making trips to the north to booksellers. At the same time, he began to live 'over the shop' in Soho Square. Three years later, he pirated a series of Biblical commentaries by the American, Rev. Albert Barnes. His brother-in-law became a partner in 1848, the name of the business then changing to Routledge and Warne and, three years after that, William's younger brother, Frederick, also joined the firm, which became Routledge and Company.

George Routledge's foresight enabled him to see the possibility of cheap books. Some of the larger publishers were no longer providing him with his stock in trade of slow-moving stock, but they reprinted such works in cheaper editions themselves. Even so, a book was still not a cheap commodity and few people were prepared to pay five or six shillings (25 or 30 pence). George's success lay in that he reduced the price to a shilling or eighteen (old) pence, thus bringing the cost within a far greater range of purchasers. Copyright, particularly of foreign books, was doubtful in those days. The firm felt that here was a useful additional source of material. In summer, 1848, he started the **Railway Library**, at incredibly low prices. Most of these were by New World authors. Indeed, seven of the first ten were by J. Fenimore Cooper, the author of 'The Last of the Mohicans'. As the series attracted attention, other out-of-copyright works by British authors began to appear and eventually, Jane Austen, Disraeli, Captain Marryat and Harrison Ainsworth agreed that their works should be re-issued. The success was astonishing.

W. H. Smith had opened the first station bookstall in Euston station in 1848 and other outlets in major stations followed. As demand grew, Smith's placed an order for a thousand copies of each new publication, which ushered in the era of mass marketing. However, pirating could not be allowed to continue and by the early 1850s, recourse to the courts cut off this lucrative trade. In spite of the rulings, some uncopyrighted issues were still made and Routledge sold over half a million copies of 'Uncle Tom's Cabin'.

In 1854, the House of Lords overturned the previous decision. Only if a foreign author actually resided in the United Kingdom could his or her copyright be secure. American writers asked for large sums of money to allow their books to be printed and sold, but the reversal meant that their works were no longer 'theirs'. In the same year, Routledge opened a branch office in New York to gain better access to new American works

In 1855, Maria, the mother of eight children, died and three years later, he married Mary Grace Bell, by whom there were to be two more children. In that decade, he was the leader in publishing illustrated books. There was another slight hiccup when it was decided that foreigners could claim copyright if they were resident in the British Empire at the time of publication. Routledge moved quickly and took full advantage of this new situation. He persuaded Longfellow to remain in England long enough for his 'New England Tragedies' to be published in London before the book appeared in the USA. For this, Longfellow received £1000.

As long as George Routledge was actively involved in the firm, it never left the successful track of cheap reprints, which had assured his fortune. Towards the end of the 1880s, he spent more and more time in Cumberland and less running the business, finally retiring in 1887. He had published some 5000 volumes, two a week, since he started fifty years ago. He died in December, 1888, leaving the running of the business to his two sons, Robert and Edmund.

In spite of various swings of fortune, the firm is still in existence today, with a strong reputation in the field of academic publishing.

THE MARKET PLACE and HIGH CROSS STREET

The Market Place has seen many changes over the past fifty years. Half of the north side was cleared and, in place of the dilapidated buildings, a brand new home for old people has been constructed. In 2001, the shops which had been part of the ground floor level of this redevelopment were converted to provide a new library for the town, replacing the very cramped premises in Front Street, the previous site that had been in use since the Library had been moved into the town centre. Before, it had been housed in one wing of the old workhouse reception building in Union Lane: the School Clinic occupied the northern wing.

One picture that has survived shows the rear of the buildings, the old shops and public houses, of the northerly side of the Market Place in a tumbledown condition.

The building on the right of the picture, with the wall bowing alarmingly, is the rear of what had been Farish's drapery store. This faces on to High Cross Street. Later, it became Richardson's, then Jackson's, then an ironmonger's run by the Tunnicliff brothers, before being converted into a flower shop, the 'Daisy Chain'. This occupies the

49

ground floor, with the Jackson Court flats on the upper floors.

A late 19th century picture of Jackson and Son

The tall building with the large chimney-stack is Jackson's draper's shop. From this aspect, it has hardly changed. It is the property to the left that was demolished. In days gone by, there was a dairy here and also a mineral water works belonging to Armstrong's.

The front of the old buildings can be seen in this postcard of the 1950s, with a 'United' bus awaiting its next journey, It was the common habit for these buses to be parked on the cobbles, often for some time. Note the old gas lamp and the two flagpoles – there is only one there now. In the cobbles in front of the Moot Hall, there are now floodlights installed. The Hall is illuminated at times during the year. The second little gable is Smith's shop and, behind and above the awning, is an advertisement for Hovis bread. The 'Joiner's Arms' stood on the corner of the square leading out to Wellmeadow Terrace. Nearer to Jackson's shop, which occupied a prominent position on the left of the picture, was a temperance hotel. Unfortunately, the picture is not sharp enough to allow the names of the shops on the eastern aspect of the square to be read.

On the south side of the square stood Stamford House, a Georgian building that had been a bank, amongst other things. One of the occupiers was the Misses Latimer, whose family were carters. They kept a stable with some twenty horses on Moatside. Stamford House was demolished about 1970. It was a very distinguished building, but had fallen into a state of very serious disrepair. It was a great shame that the façade could not have been saved, as its replacement, a 'Fine Fare'

supermarket, did nothing to enhance either the grace or the beauty of the square. This is a building that has also changed hands on several occasions, having belonged to Somerfields, Gateway and now Spar, who completely refurbished the building when they took it over.

This photograph shows it in its 'Gateway' days, before the cobbles were removed and a parking bay created. There was some outcry about the stones' being replaced, but the general consensus is that there is danger on the cobbles, particularly for older folks, but they were part of Brampton's heritage! It must be assumed that this picture was taken on a Sunday morning. Usually, one can hardly move for parked cars on any other day!

The little shop to the left of 'Gateway', now a fruit and vegetable retailer, was for many years a watchmaker and jeweller's by the name of Reed. Most of the other shops along the north side of the square, visible behind the light car, have also changed hands. The only one remaining in the same owner's possession since this was taken is Cranston's the butchers, previously Waugh's, immediately to the right of the street light. The picture is of unknown date, but probably in the early part of the 1990s.

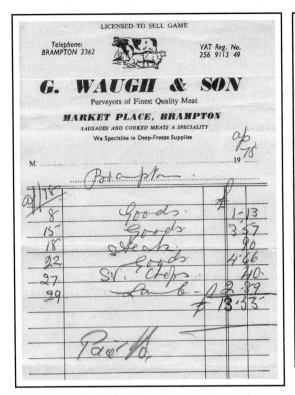

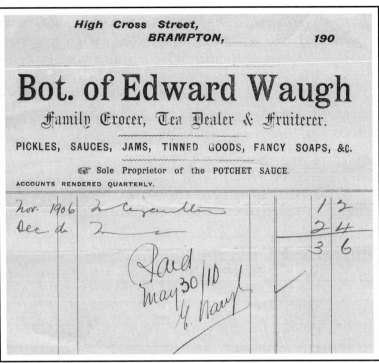

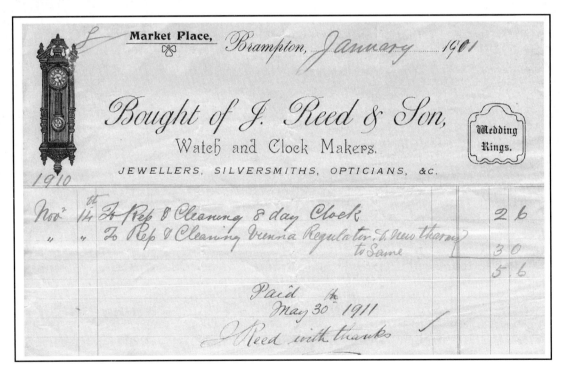

I have been fortunate to be loaned many old billheads from about ninety years ago, which present a very different image of the town in those days. The other bill is from Waugh the grocer, whose shop stood on the corner of High Cross Street and the Market Place, is a shop that changed ownership about 1911. It is clearly shown on the picture of the Coronation procession for George V (the front cover illustration of 'Brampton, Old and New') but on a photograph of Jackson's drapery shop of 1912 or 1913, it had vanished to be replaced by the shop front we now see as part of Green Design's offices. The sum of 3/6, which equates to $17\frac{1}{2}$p, would have bought very many cigarettes in 1906. For many years, Wills' 'Woodbine' cigarettes cost one old penny for five!

One of the surprising features of these old accounts is for how long the traders were prepared to extend credit for goods supplied. The bill from Edward Waugh, for instance, shows that the cigarettes had been supplied in November and December, 1906, but the account was not settled until May, 1910. This is a far cry from today, when threats of debt recovery come scarcely a month after the goods have been delivered!

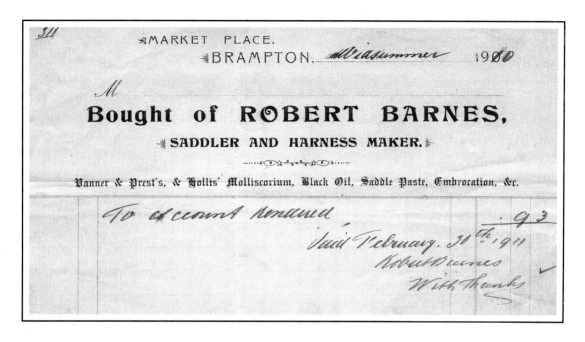

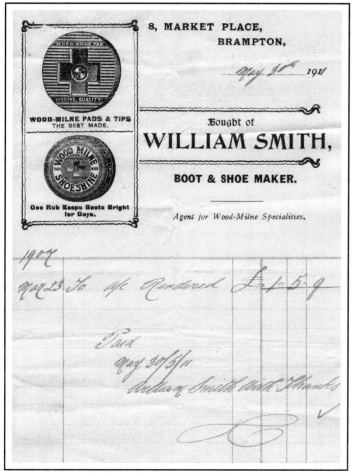

Robert Barnes waited eight months for his money! In 1910, his business was in the Market Place, but by 1929, he is shown as trading from 26, High Cross Street, which is now occupied by the Chinese takeaway.

William Smith also waited four years for settlement. One can only assume that there must have been some very compelling reason for so long a delay.

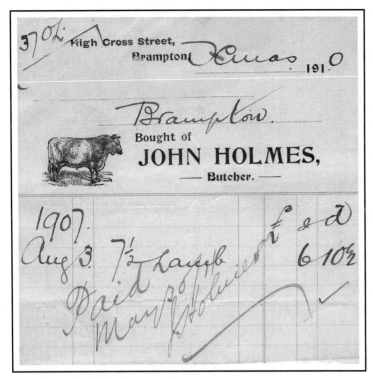

Holmes' butcher's shop was one of three listed in the town at the end of the Edwardian era – the others were Murray's in Main Street and Blaylock's in the Market Place.

The whole list of occupants of trade premises in High Cross Street leads to serious thought as to where they could all have carried on their businesses! There was a baker (Miss Jane Barker), an artificial teeth maker (Mr. William R. Bott), who came on Wednesdays, a solicitor's office, (Cartner and Milburn), a milliner (Miss Priscilla Hetherington, whose shop was where the 'Jacobite' café now stands) two boot and shoemakers, (Couch's and Pattinson's), a chemist (Mr. Gaddes, although this could be construed as being on Main Street), a district surveyor of highways and buildings (Mr. John Mark), two ironmongers (Milburn's and Routledge's), a tailor (Mr. Edward Reay), a draper (Thomas Richardson), a hotel, a cycle maker (Mr. John Shipley), and three grocers (Thomas Park, Thompson Brothers and Edward Waugh). Of these, one shoe shop (Hamilton's) and the hotel (the 'White Lion') are still extant. Naturally, other shops have taken the places of those older traders.

It must be remembered that there was a central block of shops in High Cross Street, which effectively closed off the junction on to Main (Back) Street. Of the enterprises listed above, three were contained in that group (Reay's, Routledge's and Shipley's)

Jamieson's the plumbers and Burton's the drapers were the other two businesses in that central block when it was demolished at the end of the 1920s.

I have saved until last an account that gives the lie to the theory that all ourforebears wrote in copperplate handwriting! Maybe it is because chemists must be experts at deciphering the medical profession's script that Mr. Younger was tempted to copy them! The facsimile is enlarged about one and a half times to make the exercise of reading it somewhat easier, but even then, it is no simple matter!

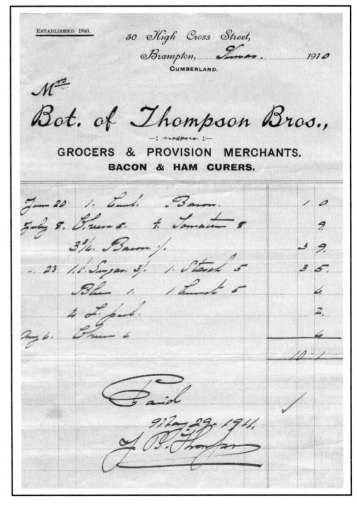

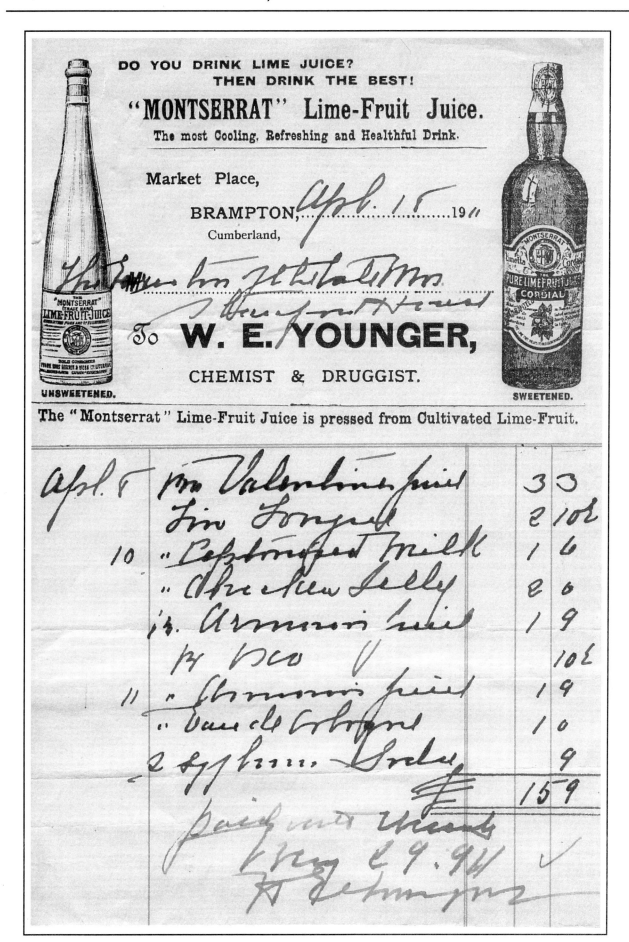

PETER BURN,
THE BRAMPTON POET.

On the wall of the Moot Hall is a plaque that commemorates a man, deeply respected by his fellow townspeople, Peter Burn. He has another memorial, too, in the form of a book of poetry, which runs to almost 400 pages. It is simply called 'Poems'.

Peter Burn's father, also named Peter, was a market gardener in the town. His address is given as Front Street in the 1829 Trades Directory. Peter, the son, was apprenticed to a draper in Hull, in the

Zion Chapel before its conversion into flats

East Riding of Yorkshire. Whilst he was there, he became a devout Congregationalist, with particular regard for one of the divines of that church, a man called John Pulsford. He dedicated an early edition of his poems to this man and later, named his son after him. After his apprenticeship was completed, he had a draper's shop in Leyburn, in the North Riding. When he returned to his home town, he opened a business in the shop which is now the Chinese takeaway in Front St.

He was an active member of the Zion Independent Chapel, a building, now converted into flats, that still survives immediately between the strangely-named "Oddfellows' Arms" and the present United Reformed Church. Upon the closure of his chosen place of worship, he transferred to Presbyterian membership. He was a very broad-minded man – today, he would be described as 'ecumenical' – and for some time, he served Rev. Henry Whitehead, once Vicar of Brampton, as a lay reader in the Lanercost Parish. Two or three years after Whitehead's death, Burn published a short tract entitled 'Reminiscences of the late Henry Whitehead, a Non-conformist's tribute to a Churchman'. It is clear, from Burn's fulsome tribute, that here was a man years ahead of his time in the quest for all men to be brothers. The Vicar's life and service is commemorated in the Apostles' window in St. Martin's, the pane referred to in the last stanza of the poem. In addition to his work at Lanercost, Peter Burn was always ready to help both the Vicar and the community in many ways. The poem, which Burn wrote as a tribute in that booklet, shows the affection in which Rev. Henry Whitehead was held.

One heaven we sought, yet walked apart
As strangers, until Whitehead came;
He taught us love is not in name,
But has its kingdom in the heart

To limit creed with him was sin,
He gloried in sufficiencies;
He bridged our little differences
And made us feel we are akin.

The life that is – the life to be
Were unto him two verities;
He lived to each and now he sees
His wisdom in Eternity.

His was a love of brotherhood –
He lived the man, by word and deed;
In pictured pane, our sons shall read
Of him we loved, who lived to good.

Burn's poems were issued in a series of collections from 1860 onwards. Many deal with local topics and places: they are often accompanied by lengthy footnotes, giving much detail of local history. In the last decade of the nineteenth century, he gave lectures to audiences at the Central Hall, Brampton, which were later published by Isaac Hodgson in a little booklet called 'Fireside Crack'.

It is a fascinating volume to read. There are eye-witness accounts of life in Brampton in the 1830s, a life which has long gone, almost beyond our comprehension, yet here is a man who not only saw it, but still had a sufficiently vivid recollection of his days as a child, coupled with the vision and the oratorical skill to make the past come alive once more. There are also descriptions of some of the local characters, wonderfully drawn and described, with all their little idiosyncrasies!

Peter Burn died in 1902. His friends placed the memorial plaque on the Moot Hall, stating that it was in recognition of his service to the common good - 'A good name is rather to be chosen than great riches'. He is not a well-recognised figure as a poet. To the people of Brampton, though, he is of great interest and deserves to be better known. His poems tell of border legends, local ghost stories and familiar places such as Hell Beck, Lanercost, Naworth, Abraham's Cave, the Written Rock and the Capon Tree. People of the town and district also provided inspiration: Belted Will Howard, Bonnie Prince Charlie, Charles Howard, Joseph Coulthard, the schoolmaster, who founded Croft House Academy and, of course, Lizzie Baty, the Brampton Witch, a story about whom was told in 'Brampton, Old and New'.

Peter Burn's Memorial tablet on the Moot Hall.

One of his works makes a convenient link to the next topic.

"THE DANDY"

This poem, written in 1880, was published in his book "Autumn Leaves" in 1885 and refers to the old horse-drawn vehicle which ran from the coal staithes near the foot of Station Road to Brampton Junction station. It connected there with the trains of the North Eastern Railway.

When holidays and school began,
I rode within the little van,
That with and without horses ran,
  And strangely named 'The Dandy'.

Great changes have been wrought since then –
The telegraph outruns the pen,
The telephone, the tongues of men –
  Yet still we have 'The Dandy'.

Full forty years have had their run –
I've had my share of work and fun,
I've seen strange things beneath the sun,
  But none to match 'The Dandy'.

The town is small – so shall it be:
It had, and has, its thousands three
It talks and dreams prosperity!
  Its nightmare is 'The Dandy'.

The railway leaves us in the cold,
Directors name a grievance old:
Are we for ever to be told –
  Your Granddads chose 'The Dandy'?

Let this pervade their money-plan –
Man lives to serve his brother man!
Then blessings shall replace the ban –
  The train supplant 'The Dandy'.

Our grand-dames had the old pack-horse,
Then came the dogcart in its course:
Now youngsters mount the iron horse
  And Brampton runs its 'Dandy'!

The Dandy Coach

Burn adds the note to his 1901 edition: "On Monday, July 4th, 1881, the 'Dandy' was superseded by a powerful tank locomotive engine, bearing the name 'Dandie Dinmont'. But a few years, however, and 'Dandie Dinmont' ceased serving us and today transit is by bus between Brampton and Brampton Junction. Our thanks are due to the Howard Arms and Bush Hotel proprietors for service rendered to us in that respect."

At that time, Brampton people thought that prosperity would depend on a better link with the railway and, after many years of pressure, the North Eastern Railway did reinstate the Dandy line as a branch line in 1913 and called the old coal staithe station 'Brampton Town'. This was also very shortlived (only ten years) and, for nearly eighty years, 'The Dandy' has come to mean the green track on which these varied vehicles once ran.

However, there were grandiose schemes!

THE BRAMPTON LIGHT RAILWAY.
WE MIGHT HAVE HAD TRAMS!

The relative remoteness of the railway station to the centre of Brampton was an issue that had occupied the deliberations of the town's residents for many years. There were several reasons for its situation and attempts were made over the years to do something about the matter. It was suggested that the North Eastern Railway should build a diversion to bring the line nearer to the town centre, with a station in the Craw Hall area, but the directors would have none of it. The length of line needed and the cost involved would have been out of all proportion to the benefits gained.

One of the more exotic plans was for a tramway. That this idea was taken seriously by the Parish Council is in no doubt. This would have become the Brampton Light Railway. The newspaper report of the time is interesting, as it deals with other proposals, such as the widening of Lovers' Lane, assuming that the land for that purpose had been

Public feeling ran very high at this time and the matter was taken seriously. It isn't known who this citizen is, but his protest was clear enough: GIVE US THE LIGHT RAILWAY. HERE'S THE MAYOR.'
The photograph is taken at the Craw Hall end of Lovers' Lane

available. (It wasn't – the owner, a Mrs. Wilkinson, had refused to sell.) Lord and Lady Carlisle were keenly interested in the scheme and the alternative routes that were suggested by the engineers. The Council representatives were Mr. Jackson and Mr. Lee, and they made their report to the other members:

"We beg to report that we had an interview with Lord and Lady Carlisle at Naworth Castle on Monday 21st September, when the proposed light railway between Brampton and Brampton Junction was fully discussed. The report of Mr. Harrison, the engineer, was carefully considered, together with the various routes that have been suggested. An opinion was expressed that, while it was desirable that a tram line should go through the town as far as the Magistrates' Office (which was in the Police Station), if possible, the routes suggested, via High Cross Street or Main Street, were narrow in places and in this respect might cause some inconvenience and that a more convenient route might be found by the widening of Lovers' Lane and thus proceed to the town by the Market Place and Front Street. It was decided that enquiries should be made as to the feasibility of this scheme. It was also suggested that to lessen the expenditure by purchase of land, the line might be extended from the terminus of the present Dandy line through the vacant ground at the Coal Staithes and thus gain access to Station Road at the top of the Sands near the staithes. The depot might then be either at the Coal Staithes or at the low end of town."

In a short discussion that followed, Mr. George Smith asserted that any scheme that did not go round the town and practically did away with the buses was not worth considering. Mr. Lee said that it had been suggested to bring the line down to the Moat Side or near Oval House at the first. Mr. Penfold said that the streets might be narrow, but the trams would only be allowed to travel at a certain speed through the town. Mr. Lee thought they should obtain powers to go right round the town, even if they did not do it at first. The Chairman said that would leave it open to some future time. Mr Lee: Yes, and if the line was paying well, we might extend it. Mr. Cheesbrough favoured making the line right round the town. If they brought the line by way of Craw Hall and Front Street to the Police Station, they would leave out the whole of Moat Side and Moat Street, which would not be satisfactory. Mr. Harding and Mr. J. Smith thought it would be much better if they could have a service to all parts of the town. The Chairman said that they had better make enquiries as to the new route and, if the owners would be willing to sell the land required and agree on something to put before a public meeting. Mr. Lee had agreed to make the necessary enquiries. Further discussion of the subject was postponed.

There the matter rested, as it still does!

FRONT STREET.

This picture is part of a much larger one, but it has been cropped to draw attention to the 'Coffee Tavern'. This business was run by Hamilton Harding. It occupied the premises that had previously been occupied by the 'Shepherd's Inn'. This hostelry had brought its Inn sign across the road from the corner of the Howard Arms Lane at some period in the nineteenth century and gave its name to Shepherd's Lane, which, in 2001 was dignified by the addition of one of the new street-name plates. Amy Harding, Hamilton's granddaughter, tells that during the winter, the children of the town would warm their hands against the tavern wall, where it was heated by the cooking range. This picture was probably taken on a Wednesday, the market day of long-standing, the assumption based on the large number of carts visible. At other times, virtually no wheeled vehicles would be seen.

One of the characteristics of Front Street is that the overall appearance has changed relatively little. The names above the shops might change over the years, but apart from the radical refurbishment of the Co-operative store, the aspect remains largely unchanged.

Front Street, probably about 1920

Sometime in the early 1950s, Dickinson's furniture shop 'grew' an extra storey. A postcard view of the 1940s clearly shows a two-storey building, with the Co-operative Stores drapery department next door. Today, it has three storeys. It is now the 'Discount Warehouse', having previously been owned by Clive Brown of Haltwhistle. The much earlier view shows the street mercifully free of traffic.

March, 2002

The Howard Arms Lane was a 'dead end', giving access to the rear of the houses on the south side of Front Street and providing pedestrian access to the bowling green. There was a blacksmith's forge in these buildings, owned in 1901 by Mr. Todd and later by Mr. Armstrong. Blacksmiths were probably as important as any other people in the community, not merely for the shoeing of horses, but also for all manner of repairs to agricultural machinery and other implements. Later, it was used as a mineral water works run by Tom Nixon. The buildings are now converted into private housing.

In the picture on the previous page can be seen the sign indicating that there was a garage to the rear of the 'Howard Arms'. In earlier years, this had been a livery stable, run by George Bell. There was another Bell, Thomas, who is listed as a 'carriage proprietor' in the 1910 directory. It is possible that the two men could have been related.

The former blacksmith's shop in Howard Arm's Lane

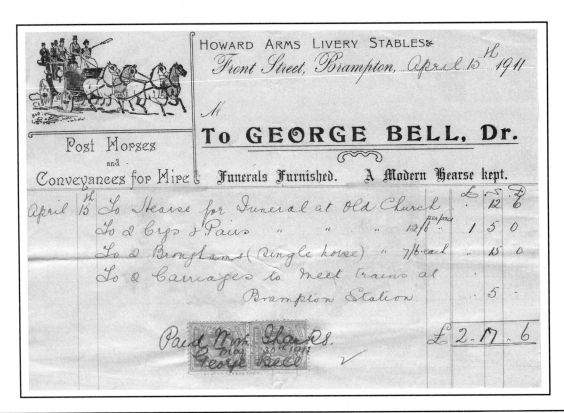

Front Street in the late 1920s

Even well on into the last century, there is little traffic to be seen in the postcards of the day. It is not easy to date this picture –from the style of the lady's fashion, it would appear to be around the late 1920s. Nixon's garage, which was badly damaged by a fire in November 1926, occupied the corner where the arch can be distinguished, but there is no sign of the garage on the picture. There is an ancient bus parked by the Moot Hall and the premises that were once the 'Half Moon' Inn shows a hooded doorway, once a common feature of the town. The Conservative Club, once the 'Black Bull', is unusual in having a 'jettied' upper floor. Both these alehouses lost their licences in

Lady Carlisle's temperance drive. There is a telephone kiosk outside the post office, in the position where there are three today.

This very old picture, which unfortunately is not very sharp, possibly dates from the time of Queen Victoria's Diamond Jubilee in 1897, shows three public houses side by side. The one to the left was (and still remains) the 'Shoulder of Mutton', the darker brick-built house was 'The Samson' and the one on the extreme right, the white building, was the 'Black Bull', the licensee of which was Senhouse Martindale Winthrop, who also had a barber's shop on the premises! The site of the 'Samson', whose licensee in 1901 was a Mr. Carrick, is now the Co-operative store.

The election day picture is probably in the 1920s. Whether this was a local or general election is not known. What is now Barclay's Bank was, in those days, the 'Bank of Liverpool and Martin's, Ltd.' A delivery bicycle is leaning against the wall.

The next picture is post World War Two – note another delivery bicycle leaning against the Conservative Club wall, once so commonplace, but an almost extinct machine nowadays. They would usually be ridden by an errand boy, nearly always whistling a popular tune of the day! By this time, the 'Bank of Liverpool and Martin's, Ltd.' had become just plain 'Martin's Bank'.

Post war Front Street

Of late, some of the shops on Front Street seem to have changed hands so very frequently that it is difficult to remember who was where! The one below is a case in point. It had been 'Brampton Sports' in the 1980s, then became in turn the 'Video Centre', 'The Halifax Building Society' and 'Homesearch' and is now preparing to open, in mid-2002, as a laundry. Perhaps the fault is mine, for not recording the various shop fronts in photographs.

This snowy day was in January, 1979, when local communications were effectively paralysed. By this date, the number of cars seen in pictures increase, until by the present day, stopping legitimately in Brampton is becoming something of a lottery!

One of the more unusual shops that the Front Street has acquired recently is 'Beanies Direct 2 U', a shop designed to stop youngsters in their tracks as they gaze entranced at the display of hundreds of soft toys. Stephen Rowe's optician's is in the shop that was formerly Carlisle's butcher's shop. The 'Capon Tree Café' has been recently refurbished, the antique shop next to that is newly opened and next door again is the 'Pristine Laundry'.

Front Street, March 2002.

The 'Beanies Direct' Interior

The two cars seen on this view of Front Street from the bottom of Gelt Road are both Morris, the front one a 'Minor'. The 'split windscreen' models were the first style of these cars to be produced. Later models, introduced in 1956 had a curved one piece screen.

This postcard view of the lower end of Front Street dates from around 1900. The Church tower was not finished until 1905, as there was no money available for completion. This provides a very useful 'dating' indication with respect to old photographs of the town.

St. Martin's Church and Hall, 1906. 'Garden Hill Cottage' is in the foreground, the only dwelling that remained after the clearance of the site for the new Hall.

The foundation stone of St. Martin's Hall was laid in the summer of 1894 by Mrs. Thompson, the widow of Colonel Thompson of Milton Hall, in whose memory it was built. The stone was raised by a pulley and, after she had spread the cement with an ivory-handled silver trowel, it was lowered carefully into position to cover a bottle placed into a hollow below the stone containing some items of relevance to the time. The design of the Hall was by Charles Ferguson of Carlisle

According to the 'Carlisle Patriot', it held an extract from the December 1893 Parish magazine, which contained details of the origins of the hall, coins of the realm, a list of officials of the church and Sunday school, the names of the building committee, the architects and the contractors, a copy of the Parish magazine for 1894, a copy of Cheesbrough's Almanac and Local Directory, local newspapers and clippings, the balance sheet of the Bazaar, a list of the Rowing Club members and officials, the Volunteers' card for August, Cricket and Football teams' cards, the Agricultural Society's balance sheet and a list of members, the Literary and Field Naturalist Society card, the Oddfellows' Society balance sheet and membership list, the Floral and Horticultural Society's catalogue, notices about the Boys' Brigade and the County Court, photographs of the Vicar, Colonel Thompson and the site of the Hall before removal of the old houses and a copy of the current 'Ancient and Modern' hymnbook.

St. Martin's Hall, 1970

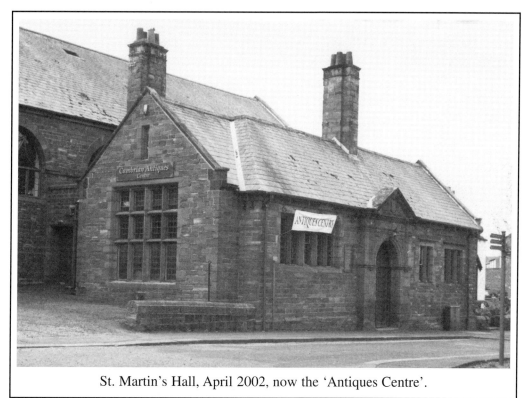

St. Martin's Hall, April 2002, now the 'Antiques Centre'.

After a period of financial difficulty, the Hall was used as a sports hall, during which time the stage was removed. This venture also failed and its present use is as an antiques centre. It has been sympathetically altered and now presents a series of 'rooms' in which the traders can display their goods.

One of the display areas in the refurbished St. Martin's Hall

A long-case clock by
Cairns of Brampton

A close-up of the clock face. Cairns is
mentioned in the section on Main Street,
where he had his workshop.

GELT ROAD - THE LONNING

Gelt Road is a part of Brampton that has seen great changes. The old property at its foot was swept away in 1968 to be replaced by the new, which quickly earned the nickname 'Jerusalem',

because of the flat roofs of the house and their many differing levels. I suppose that, over the past years, we have become accustomed to its alien colour – it no longer seems to intrude as it did when it was first presented.

A small and regrettably indistinct photograph was loaned to me several years ago. It had been taken from the field just below Irthing Valley School looking southeast. In the foreground can be seen a long-gone row of cottages and the tannery and, above its roof, 'Garden Hill Cottage'. Behind that again is the roof of St. Martin's Hall and then the roofs of the little houses that lined Gelt Road. The curved roof of the joiner's shop can just be made out, only one of the few buildings which remain of those that stood at the bottom end of the road. (The others are the hardware store in the old Methodist Chapel and the bottom house on the right.)

Unfortunately, there are only a few photographs of the lower end. Folk memory tends to forget just what was there, but there is one picture, very battered, that I was lucky enough to be able to copy. Bella Haines is standing with her foot on the kerb and Maggie Heslop is the girl wearing the light coat. The third girl cannot be named. The photograph was taken outside that house that stood immediately adjacent to the joiner's works and lower down the hill. The splendid gas lamp is held on a somewhat insubstantial bracket, with the supplying pipe running exposed up the house wall, a form of construction which would be frowned on today as contravening Health and Safety regulations. Further down the hill can be seen another figure. (This must be a man - girls rarely wore trousers in those days, although the unnamed girl does!) He is leaning against the low wall of the small garden, which a few of the houses possessed. It was in one of these that Nurse Griffiths lived.

The Harrison family: Thomas, George, Mary, Margaret, Jane junior and Jane

The Harrison family, shown in this magnificent photograph, which dates from about 1857, lived at 'West View', a house that was rebuilt in 1858. Thomas Harrison (1814-1899) was the founder of the grocer's shop that was a feature of Front Street for many years. He married Jane Elliott (1825-1908) at Hayton parish church on Christmas Day, 1848. They are seen here with their first four children, Margaret, (1849-1931) who married Thomas Bird; George Arthur (1851-1932), who married Isabella Hodgson; Mary (1854-1916), who married James Hetherington and Jane (1857-1953), who married Thomas Fawkes. There were to be three other children, all of whom lived to be over ninety.

The little row of four cottages at the very top of Gelt Road, next to the Aaronstown Lonning, is now divided into four separate dwellings, two on the ground floor and two on the first.

It might be surprising to know that this was, at one time, actually split into eight! There is clear evidence of this in the little building behind the row, where eight doors can be seen, which provided storage space for the inhabitants. To say that conditions must have been cramped is to understate the situation!

Solway View, March 2002.

Storage shed behind Solway Veiw, March 2002.

Aaronstown from the footpath to Wreay Farm, 1990. Depending on which gazetteer you read, the name of the cluster of houses would appear to be the first in the alphabetical list of place names of Britain!

Although the Capon Tree was mentioned in "The Changing Face of Brampton", it still provokes questions about the name and purpose. I was given an old newspaper cutting some time ago, in which the subject was discussed – it makes interesting reading. The writer suggests that the tree was an oak. This must be conjectural, as the tree was already a battered ruin in 1833, when Ford did a sketch of it. The avenue of beech trees along Capon Tree Road, now very much past their best in many cases, is about 180 years old, on the evidence of the counting of their rings when the more 'dangerous' ones have been felled. In any case, if the origin of the name is of a 'capping tree', that is, one used for hangings, none of the trees would have been anything like mature enough to serve that purpose.

Hutchinson, the historian of Cumberland, seems to have been responsible for the tradition that the Assize judges took refreshment under its shade. He wrote, 'At Irthing, or Ruleholme Bridge, the High Sheriff of the county meets the Judges of Assize to escort them to Carlisle. The Under Sheriff attends them from the county boundary at Temon. Tradition says that, as the judges and their retinue could not be properly accommodated with provisions on their way from Newcastle to Carlisle, they were under the necessity of taking capons, etc., with them. On these, they regaled themselves under a large oak tree, yet growing (1794) on the estate of John Hetherington, Esq., by the road leading from Brampton to Warwick Bridge. It is called the Capon Tree and has apparently withstood the blasts of several hundred years.'

Whilst it is possible that the Capon Tree was used as a regular resting place for the judges, the explanation seems unsatisfactory. It leaves out of account the fact that there are other Capon Trees in the area, notably near Jedburgh and Alnwick. One suggestion for the name is that it could be derived from the game of 'kep' or 'keppy ball', supposedly played by girls beneath its shade. Another is that it is a corruption of 'covyne' or 'convoy', a place where the host might convoy his departing guests. Others suggest it is from a different source, the Scottish word 'kep', to meet for the settlement of questions of local government. The author of the article offers another tentative solution, that the word might be used as it is in 'Capernwray' in North Lancashire, where the word has the meaning of 'merchant' or 'chapman'. The trees mentioned above, including Brampton's, are all on trading routes and could have been places where the travelling merchants met. (Capon Tree Road was, at one time, the high road from Carlisle to Newcastle.)

Whatever the origin of the name, there was, in the past, no doubt about the popularity of the Capon Tree as a place of meeting. Lovers would meet there, bargains would be concluded and fights arising from disputes in the market would be settled under the old tree.

It was, though, the scene of tragedy after the failure of Prince Charles Edward's abortive attempt to recapture the English throne for the Stuart dynasty. Ruthless vengeance was meted out to those who had borne arms in his cause. Twenty were 'partially' hanged at Carlisle and then disembowelled, another six at Penrith and, on October 21st, 1746, six more suffered a similar fate at Brampton. The choice of the town was, in some ways, appropriate. It had seen the activities of the Prince and his generals when the Mayor and Corporation of Carlisle were forced to surrender the city's keys on bended knee.

No doubt the Government of the day decreed that it was good policy to demonstrate to the population at large that the Young Chevalier's enterprise had turned into utter failure and to create the impression that no quarter would be given to those who might seek, in the future, to restore the Stuarts.

After so dread an event, the tree acquired a sinister reputation and it became the centre for many local ghost stories, among others that the unhappy prisoners could be seen dangling from the branches. As if accursed, the tree declined, helped by visitors who cut pieces of it away as souvenirs! It has completely disappeared, but several local people, including Mr. Henry Penfold, were instrumental in setting up the existing memorial to those who died so brutal a death there.

SPORT

As with other communities, Brampton has played sport of many kinds, from the seemingly legal warfare of rugby, through rowing on the Tarn, a subject that has been mentioned in earlier books, to the stately pursuit of bowls, but even this leisurely game has its moments of aggression! Brampton's Bowling Club is claimed to be the fourth oldest in the country, having been founded in 1761. Naturally, the bicentenary was celebrated in style, with matches played between people in both Georgian and Victorian costume, as well as those in contemporary dress. It would appear, from the memories recalled, that the rules of the competition were extremely elastic!

Today, the Club remains a progressive organisation and a new bower was recently built to provide excellent and modern facilities. It was opened in 1996. The green and bower were pictured in May 2002. The houses in the background are those of Showfield, a housing estate that dates from 1982.

The New Bower.

Referring to the 1925 guidebook, Clive Taylor was the secretary of the Brampton Football Club. They played in the first division of the Carlisle and District League and had won the Carlisle Charity Shield in the 1923/4 season. The club claimed to have 'an excellent playing pitch at Cote Hill Park, five minutes walk from the town'. Through the years, there have been many photographs of football teams, but unfortunately, many of the players' names cannot now be recalled, as with this picture of the Brampton XI who were the winners, in 1928, of the Carlisle and District League 2nd Division. The picture would seem to have been taken at Brunton Park, the home of Carlisle United.

Back row: Tom Armstrong; John Simpson; Jacob Milburn; Jim Dicker; Robbie Atkinson; Freddie Spencer; Bob Edger.
Front Row: Billy Bell; Jackie Hope; Arthur Atkinson; Unknown; Reg Atkinson; Arnold Hodgson.

The town's cricket team is Irthing Vale Wanderers. Again, several pictures of the team have come to light, which were published in the excellent history of the club, written by Alf Morris in 1993.

IRTHING VALE WANDERERS CRICKET CLUB, 1966.

Back Row: R. Biggins, R. Potts, F. Bright, G. Thompson, D. Bright, L. Clifford.
Front Row: M. Brodie, W. Walker, D. Wall (captain), I. Farish, R. McClelland.

Arthur Ruell at Beckriggs, about 1929. The grass was not as long as this on the square!

Bob Murray, pictured after scoring 118 at Castle Howard during the tour of 1929

Arthur Ruell was the professional and the coach to the team for twelve years from 1923. When he joined the Club, he was already over forty years old. At the same time, another younger man joined, by the name of Bob Murray. In Ruell's first season, Irthing Vale reached the final of the Carlisle Knockout competition and he was awarded the gold medal for the best batting performance. During his years with the club, he scored one century, seventeen half-centuries and on three occasions, he took all ten wickets in an innings. In 1928, he took 10 for 16, including a hat trick. This is a record that speaks for itself! Bob Murray and Ruell dominated the closing years of the 1920s and the early 1930s. Murray scored 140 not out in 90 minutes in the Carlisle Knockout Competition and, in 1932, he went even better by scoring 148 out of a total of 204 against Scotby. This remains the highest score ever made by an Irthing Vale player to this day.

Regrettably, no photographs of tennis clubs have ever come to light. A 1925 guidebook tells us that the Tennis Club had two courts in the close proximity of the town. Miss Connie Murray, a butcher in the town, was their secretary. There was also a public hard court at Low Beck Side, midway between the town and the tarn. This was owned by Mr. and Mrs. Sowerby, and the remains, now overgrown with birch trees, can still be seen by the roadside across from the cottage.

L to R: Raymond Wright, Betty Riddell, Violet Wilkinson, Raymond Wright's brother, Lizzie ?? (surname unknown), Mary Stobbart, unknown girl.

L to R: unknown; Philip Milburn; Raymond Wright; Betty Riddell; Violet Wilkinson and Raymond Wright's brother.

This modern picture, taken in April 2002, tells its own story!

Swimming at the Tarn is not the regular pastime that it once was. In fact, it is actively discouraged. Generations of Brampton children must have learnt here and must have used the Bathing Hut, which appears on a number of pictures. These pictures are undated, but to avoid insulting anyone who is still alive, I shall not chance a guess! They show several of the youngsters from the town, clearly a group of friends, sitting outside the bathing hut. The two photographs were taken at the same time.

Violet Wilkinson's mother kept a sweet shop. This was at 46, Front Street, where Tom Nixon's former and vegetable business was. The father had a fish and chip shop where the Card Centre now trades. Betty Riddell's father was the secretary to the Naworth Coal Company. He had originally come from Wishaw in Lanarkshire. My informant told me that Raymond Wright's brother married Flo Nixon. Does this help anyone to remember his name?

Left to right: Willie Laird; Karen Mark; Paul Scott; Martin Brown; the Tennent's Lager Publicity Rep.; David Scott; John Kershaw; Graham Mark; Kelvin Carruthers; Derek Carruthers; Philip Corrie.

In 1977, a group of youngsters from the Tarn Rowing Club took part in a competition sponsored by Tennent Caledonian Breweries on the Clyde at Glasgow Green. The participants are shown here with their trophies.

THE BYPASS

After long deliberations about the line of the bypass, initially proposed in the 1930s, the Ministry of Transport decided that the logical route would pass to the south of the town. There were many people who felt very strongly that a northern road would have been a better solution, thus enabling traffic for Longtown to have been removed from the town, taking away even more hazards from Brampton's narrow streets. Hence, despite the narrowness and manifest unsuitability of the Irthing Bridge at Walton Lane End, now protected by traffic lights, there is still a flow of very heavy vehicles along the Main Street.

In many ways, the Highways Department did their work well. The road is visible only from a few houses. There will be many who are very aware of the constant noise, despite the road's being a cutting for a considerable distance, especially from heavy goods vehicles grinding their way up the steep gradient eastbound from the roundabout on the A69. One matter, which will be debated for a long time, is why the road wasn't made into a dual carriageway from the outset, a question that also arises with the Haltwhistle bypass some twelve miles to the east. It was finally opened in April, 1991.

This picture, taken in February 1986 looking south from 'Brookside',
is of the Castle Carrock road before the bypass bridge was built.

A corresponding picture, taken in March, 2002, with the bypass bridge.

THE TARN

The Tarn itself has been the subject of many photographs over the years. Here are two pictures dated 1893 of the original rowing boats and the Boathouse, some of which have only very recently been 'retired'. The snow scene is most probably 1895, the year of the Great Frost, when the Tarn had ice over a foot thick, so enabling a curling match to be played between England and Scotland. (Scotland won!)

Landing Stage — Talkin Tarn

It must also have been the topic for scores of postcards, four of which are reproduced here. One was dated and sent in 1903, although the illustration would have been taken long before.

The boathouse near the present day entrance to the Country Park has the doors open – clearly, the boat that normally occupied that berth is out.

Tarn End Hotel was, by 1905, when the postcard was stamped, a temperance hotel. The small jetty in the grounds was obviously in regular use at that time – it was well-maintained.

The small boathouse on the south bank was, at one time, used as a 'holiday let'. This post card is in mint condition, so there is no clue to be gained from any text or date-stamp. The path is merely a grassy track, lacking the sturdy fences, which now divide the way, with kissing gates provided for access.

Lastly, there are two photographs taken on February 17th,1985, on one of the rare occasions when there was sufficient thickness and quality of ice to allow skaters to use the Tarn safely. The winters of the present day never seem to match the severity of those of our childhood!

ENTERTAINMENT,
or 'WHAT CAN WE DO THIS WEEKEND?'

In some respects, it is astonishing what has survived from bygone days. I am not merely discussing photographs, those 'time machines' that give such penetrating insights into the appearance not only of the buildings of the town, but also of the people: their mode of dress, their way of life and facial features that enable familial likenesses to be recognised over a period of years.

Some time ago, a gentleman of the town, knowing of my pursuit of knowledge about old Brampton, presented a large envelope, which he solemnly declared would interest me. Inside were about fifteen old playbills that advertised presentations at St. Martin's Hall. In these days of instant 'entertainment' from the television (a dubious description!), the radio, the cinema, DVDs and videotapes, it is easy to forget that our forebears had none of these things. Leisure was mainly homemade in the Victorian era and earlier. The church played a major part in their social life. One could walk on a Sunday – anything else was frowned upon. There were also amateur dramatics and the music hall. Sunday evenings would be spent singing round the piano in the parlour, if you had one or both! Moving pictures came later, but provided a release from reality that enabled one to ride the range with cowboys and Indians, or penetrate into different class strata, be it up or down.

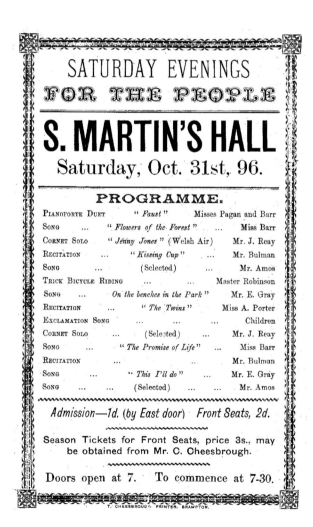

Some of these bills are reproduced here, along with a list of the films to be shown at the Brampton Cinema in November, 1951. At the children's matinees, the adventures of 'Flash Gordon' and other serials, which always finished at a most dangerous and life threatening moment, would be avidly followed by the faithful! The offerings in those days, fifty years ago, had a naiveté and innocence that is sadly lacking in today's films, but this is not the place for a moral discussion. Think of the provision made for our ancestors' pleasure, half a century, a whole century past. We may smile, perhaps a little wistfully, for those days that have passed down the long corridor of years gone by!

"Elma" must have been a popular presentation – it had been shown before on more than one occasion in the early part of the twentieth century. Does anyone have a copy of the script?

S. MARTIN'S SUNDAY SCHOOL

 **DON'T FORGET**

THE ANNUAL

CONCERT

given by the Scholars in

ST. MARTIN'S HALL

on

Tuesday, March 3rd, 1908

(Shrove Tuesday).

Action Songs, Recitations, Instrumental Music.

To Conclude with the GRAND FAIRY PLAY, entitled,

"Elma, The Fairy Child."

CHARACTERS.

Elma, The Mortal	FRANCES DODD
Elma, The Fairy	MOLLY WAUGH
Moonbeam	ALICE WARWICK
Fairy Queen	HANNAH BAXTER

Chorus of Elves and Fays.

Beautiful Dresses! Splendid Scenery!

Come and Support the Children.

Doors open at 6-30. Commence at 7.

Admission 6d. each.

There were the big occasions that would bring other excitement. The observance of Queen Victoria's Golden and Diamond Jubilees have been referred to and illustrated in "Brampton, Old and New". King George V's Silver Jubilee was marked by special celebrations and programmes for that and the coronation of George VI have survived.

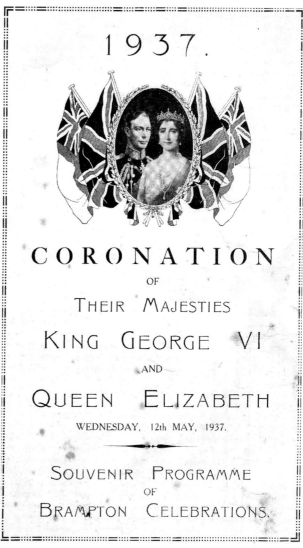

There was a full day's programme of events on May 12th, 1937, as can be read from the copy of the list on the following page. The Silver Jubilee programme was just as full, but the list of participants is not given. There will probably be instant recognition of some of the names that appear on the register of those who took part in the celebrations for the Coronation. It seems that a considerable number of the youngsters of the town took part, as well as many of the townspeople who served on the various committees. Unfortunately, few pictures of the festivities seem to have come down to us.

The 'Sands field' referred to is that which stands between The Swarthel and the Middle Road: to translate, between the Lanercost and Newcastle Roads. I am advised that the festivities were not all held on the same day, as there would have been no opportunity for the Fancy Dress competition entries in the picture shown to change from one costume to another.

PROGRAMME.

::::::::::::::::::::::::::::::::::::

7 0 a.m.   Firing of Maroons from the Moat Hill.

7 30 a.m.   Pealing of St. Martin's Church Bells.

9 30 a.m.   United Service of Thanksgiving, conducted by The Rev. E. T. Shepherd, in the Parish Church of St. Martin.

1 15 p.m.   Assembly in the Market Place of Carnival Procession.

1 30 p.m.   Headed by the Town Silver Band, the Procession moves off round the Town to the Sands.

2 30 p.m.   Judging of Classes in Sands Field.

Crowning of The Coronation Queen.

Maypole Dancing Display.

Folk Dancing.

Netball Exhibition.

5 0 p.m.   Tea and Presentation of Coronation Beakers to all Children of school age, in the Temperance Hall, by CHARLES ROBERTS, Esq., J.P.

Presentation of Coronation Mugs to all Children under school age, in St. Martin's Hall, by PULSFORD BURN, Esq.

6 0 p.m.   Sports in the Sands Field.

9 0 p.m.   Grand Coronation Dance in the Temperance Hall.

9 30 p.m.   Torchlight Procession from the Market Place round the Town to the Recreation Ground.

10 0 p.m.   Bonfire on the Recreation Ground.

CORONATION MAY QUEEN & HER COURT.

QUEEN - IRENE MITCHINSON.

Attendants—Alison Clarke, Enid Gregg, Jean Jefferson, Sheila Porter, Grace Potts, Mary Walker, Edna Shadwick.

Train Bearers—Enid Milburn, Minnie Pugh.

Crown Bearer—Ronald Milburn.

Sceptre Bearer—Alan Bird.

Heralds—Miles Atkinson, Maurice Telford.

Rose Maidens—Edith Bird, Freda Brown, Doris Cheesbrough, Joan Cheesbrough, Eleanor Corrie, Betty Finlayson, Kathleen Hetherington, Clara Hill, Davine Latimer, Violet Latimer, Jean Nelson, Nan Potts, Rita Rutherford, Elsie Stephenson, Evelyn Thompson, Nan Walker.

MAYPOLE DANCERS.

Girls Daisy Anderson, Enid Brown, Margaret Hope, Evelyn Jackson, Sheila Maclean, Ireline Mark, Gladys Pratt, Molly Storey, Gladys Taylor.

Boys Tom Andrews, Maxwell Graham, Kenneth Jackson, Vernon Neve, Ernest Pugh, Maurice Robinson, Robert Robinson, Frank Thompson, Ernest Warwick.

FOLK DANCERS.

Edna Atkinson, Jean Atkinson (extra), Olive Bell, Vera Bell, Phyllis Ewart, Betty Goodwin, May Harrison, Ada Harrison, Edith Hodgson, Alice Hoodless, Lovina Howe, Kathleen Latimer, Audrey Lawrence, Margaret Liddell, Joyce Little, Mary Mallinson, Jean Martin, Alexandra Megahy, Maureen Milbourne, Mary Nixon, Winifred O'Hara, Doris Oliphant, Jean Pratt, Ellenor Reay, Jean Ridley, Nancy Ridpath, Helen Robson, Hilda Rogers, Margaret Shadwick, Peggy Smith, Margaret Storrow, Dorothy Walker, Jean Warwick, Joyce Warwick, Christina Wylie.

Arthur Atkinson, Fergus Atkinson, Miles Atkinson, Reginald Atkinson, Robert Atkinson, Sydney Batey, William Bell, Cowan Bell, Maurice Bird, Raymond Copplestone, Leslie Corrie, Richard Dicker, John Dodd, Archibald Graham, Mark Graham, Malcolm Graham, Christopher Grindley, Herbert Harrison, Joseph Howe, Richard Howe, Frederick Lawrence, Dennis Mitchell, Peter Ridpath, Reginald Robinson, Maurice Rutherford, Arthur Scott, Raymond Simpson, Frederick Spencer, John Edward Taylor, Reginald Thompson, Harold Warwick, Thomas Wylie.

NETBALL PLAYERS.

Gladys Armstrong, Marjorie Dixon, Marjorie Errington, Emily Hetherington, Mary Hindson, Nellie Little, Audrey Newton, Violet Thomson.

Fergus Atkinson, Leslie Corrie, Richard Dicker, Frank Hutton, Dennis Mitchell, John Edward Taylor.

CORONATION PAGEANT, MAY 12TH., 1937

Back Row: Alan Bird; Enid Gregg; Jean Jefferson; Alison Clark; Miles Atkinson; Irene Mitchinson; Maurice Telford; Sheila Porter; Grace Potts; Mary Walker; Ronnie Milburn.

Second Row: Davina Latimer; Betty Finlayson; Nan Potts; Evelyn Thompson; Eleanor Corrie; Edna Shadwick; Nan Walker; Minnie Pugh; Jean Nelson; Enid Milburn.

Third Row: Doris Cheesbrough; Violet Latimer; Rita Rutherford; Edith Bird; Freda Brown.

Front Row: Elsie Stephenson; Kathleen Hetherington; Clara Hill; Joan Cheesbrough.

In May 1934, the world was astonished by the birth and survival of the Dionne Quins in Canada. For the Coronation, Brampton produced its own set of quintuplets. Even in those days, sponsorship could be obtained, as can be seen from the picture – they are advertising 'Quaker Oats'!

BRAMPTON'S QUINS!
Evelyn Thompson, Nan Walker, Lily Thompson, Nan Potts, Kathleen Pratt.

The cinema, which stood where the West Cumberland Farmers' building now is, behind Craw Hall, burnt down on June 11th, 1960. This programme, somewhat tattered but still legible, dates from November, 1951.

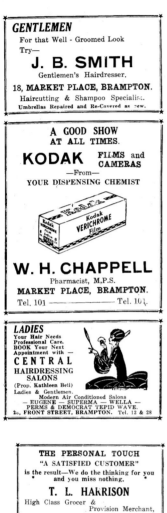

The devastation of the cinema, June 11th., 1960.

Many years ago, there was also another cinema in the town, on Gelt Road. This stood roughly where the road access to Jerusalem now is. It was a timber building with a 'tin' roof, presumably corrugated and galvanised iron. My informant said that the serial shown every Saturday was 'The Lost City'. In his recollection, it ran for years!

In the 1925 guidebook to the town, published by Harding and Irving, there is a full list of Clubs and Institutes in the town and its immediate area. This makes interesting reading. There are societies that still exist, such as the Bowling Club, the Golf Club (described in the booklet as 'Talkin Tarn Golf Club'), Irthing Vale Wanderers Cricket Club and the Brampton Angling Association. Other societies, which have lapsed over the years, also provided an opportunity for entertainment in the town.

The Chess Club 'which has a good membership', met at the Sand House Hotel (so named) every Friday evening during the winter. Mr. F. Drakeford was the Secretary, who was also the secretary of the County Association.

The secretary of the Brampton and District Motor Club was Mr. S. Shipley. It was described as an enterprising club, with an excellent fixture list of social runs and reliability trials. Their headquarters was at the Howard Arms Temperance Hotel.

There was a Brampton Choral Society, which had been in existence since 1900. They had an orchestra and over one hundred members. The guidebook entry states that they rehearse a cantata or an oratorio every winter for production at the annual concert, which was presented in early spring. The conductor was the previously mentioned Mr. F. Drakeford and the secretary was Mr. R. H. Hunter. At the present time, there are two choral societies in the town and district, the Brampton Chamber Choir and the Brampton Churches' Choir.

The Band is well documented and some of the many pictures taken of its members over the years are reproduced here.

On the awning above, one can just read '1881'. The inscription on the large drum is 'Brampton', but it is not possible to gain any further information. I do not know where the picture was taken – could it be in front of the Bowling Club bower or perhaps the station waiting shelter?

The lower picture of the band at Crosby-on-Eden Village Hall was probably taken either in the closing stages or after the end of the war - the car behind the band still has the masks on the headlights. These were designed to reduce light scatter. Whether this worked or not is a moot point! Certainly, it must have made driving incredibly difficult with the indifferent lights that cars possessed in those days.

Back row: Baxter Barnes ; Major Milne; Willie Armstrong; Ted Walker; Jim Mounsey; Billie Armstrong; George Welton senr.; George Welton junr.; Tom Armstrong.

Front row: Richard Howe; Jimmy Ruddick; John Armstrong; Laurie Armstrong; Tom Armstrong; Norman Welton (the little boy).

At least one of the faces will be very familiar in this 1983 picture, which is reproduced by kind permission of the 'Cumbrian Newspapers' group. It shows Andrew Bailey as one of the youngest members of the Band, with the two oldest members, Katie Henry and Benny Smith.

For many years, Benny was in business in the Market Place as a barber and a repairer of umbrellas. My special memory of him was his determined and upright stride as he marched down Front Street – he never seemed to walk, but always proceeded with a dignified military bearing.

Several years ago, the Band went to Spain with twenty-six musicians and brought back this certificate to commemorate their taking part in a programme that was, according to the poster, of typically English music,

The Boys' Brigade members from 1894/5 are seen here paraded in front of Green Lane House, which is now converted to an Old People's Home.

The Scout troop, about the 1920s

A group of ladies from the Conservative Club in the 1920s.

THE HAPPIEST DAYS OF YOUR LIFE...?

This letter, dated November 1854, was sent to every Parish in the Carlisle Diocese by the then Bishop of Carlisle to establish the requirements for education in the area. Most of the responses have survived, as has the one for Brampton, returned by Rev. Christopher Benson. The Bishop wrote:

My dear Sir,

Anxious to ascertain whether a better instruction might not be given to the children and whether the advantages offered by the Education Committee of the Privy Council might not be made more extensively available in this Diocese, I trouble you with the following queries, which you would oblige me by answering, with any further suggestions that you might be inclined to offer and returning the answers to me at your earliest convenience.

Yours faithfully,   *H. Carlisle.*

QUERIES

What is the number of schools in your Parish?

There is, for the labouring classes, one national School and one Infant school. Besides these, there are several private day schools and dame schools, of which latter I have no account.

State the dimensions of each school and enter the number of children it is calculated to contain.

The National (a mixed) School in 76 feet (length) by 22 feet (breadth) with another room used as a classroom a.m. and for girls' sewing p.m. 34 feet (length) by 20 feet (breadth). These rooms, according to the space required by the Privy Council, will contain 210 and 85 respectively. The Infant School will contain 90.

Average number of Pupils in actual attendance at each school.

135 average attendance Michaelmas 53 to March 54 at the National School. At the Infant School, 70 (1853-54)

Each School, whether supported by Endowment, Subscription or Quarter Pence.

By subscription and weekly pence. (The scholars paid a penny per week)

Amount of Subscriptions, Endowments and Quarter Pence received in each School, stating also the amount per quarter paid by the several pupils.

For the year ending March 4th, 1854:

National School:	Subscription:	£82.10.6	Infant School:	Subscription	about £25.0.0
	Weekly pence:	<u>£43.19.9</u>		Weekly pence	<u>9.0.0</u>
		£126.10.3			£34.0.0

Whether a Union or partial Union of the Schools in the Parish or neighbouring Parishes would be desirable, and whether possible or likely to be effected, by which a better stipend might be assigned to the Master and a larger School or Schools established.

Not desirable here.

OBSERVATIONS

We have a certificated master and three teachers in the national School and for the years 52/53, we obtained upwards of £70 towards the payment of and in augmentation of their salaries. Our schoolroom being much dilapidated, we are attempting to build new schoolrooms.

I have the honour to be, my Lord Bishop, your obedt. Servt.

C. Benson.

A National School was established in 1816 on the site now occupied by the Police Station. It was, according to Peter Burn, a long whitewashed building with a floor of clay. He tells that the boys took turns at 'claying', the post of 'clayer' being a dignified appointment! The wear and tear caused by clog irons would wreak havoc on so primitive a floor.

Joseph Coulthard, who later founded Croft House Academy, was first master and he was succeeded by Joseph Nicholson. The Vicar gave considerable oversight and attention to the school. In 1825, an Infants' School was founded in Back Street, today's Main Street. In 1847, according to the Directory, Martha Lowe was the mistress there and James Ambler and Hannah Lawson were teachers at the National School. The book also stated that a school especially for girls had been opened in 1832. Both together accommodated 200 children.

A Board School Class, 1882

Successive reports condemned the National School: the condition of the building, its stone floor (by this time), bad ventilation, lack of a playground and the poor state of the furniture. Because no improvements had been made by 1853, a circular letter was issued asking for subscriptions for a new building, informing that both the school and its site had been severely criticised by H. M. Inspectors. The plan was to sell the site and use the proceeds to erect new buildings in Moat Street.

In addition to the National Schools, the 1829 Directory lists other schools in the town as the Infants' Charity School, the Grammar School, a school run by James Graham in Oliver Square (east of the Scotch Arms Yard) and another run by James Tinling in Back Street.

In 1834, Jane Hillaby ran a Ladies' Boarding School. There was also a school at Lane Head House, Mary James' school in Front Street and Elizabeth Miller's school in Back Street.

A LADIES' SEMINARY

The caption to the 1876 drawing reads:
First schoolgirl (sweet seventeen): I am so tired of walking along two-by-two in this way! It's as bad as the animals going into the ark!

Second schoolgirl (ditto): Worse! At least, half of them were male!

In 1847, James Duncan and Mary Modlin had schools in Back Street.

By 1858, the English Presbyterian School had been founded and the Misses Randleson had a seminary in the Back Street.

By 1866, the original Infants' school in Back Street, in existence since 1825, was totally inadequate. When the lease expired, the chance was taken to close the school and a new one was built in Moat Street, opposite the National School and these buildings are still in use today as Brampton Infants' School.

In 1884, William Armstrong was running a private boys' school in the Presbyterian schoolroom, the Misses Brown had a 'middle class' school for girls in Carrick House (the present White House), Miss Jane MacQueen ran a private mixed school in Back Street and Miss Emma Sewell's ladies' academy was in the same street.

1894's directory shows Mr. James McWhirter's High School – a boarding and day school for young gentlemen and Mr. William Tucker Broad's boarding and day school for young ladies and gentlemen was in the College, 'Westwood', Station Road. Miss MacQueen's school was now in Gill Place.

School photographs seem to survive with less damage than any other pictures. Certainly, over the years, virtually all the series that was taken at the Council School in 1927 have come together. The interested response to old school classes has been remarkable. For that reason, there is no apology for the number that now follow. In several cases, it has been possible to name the children, whereas in others, they must sadly remain totally anonymous. There is always the hope that someone may recognise the figures from long years past, maybe a grandparent or other relative.

The more recent ones tend to show happier faces. Is this a tribute to enlightened teaching or are the photographers more competent in getting the children to relax?

This school class seems to be Edwardian, from the children's style of dress, with some of the boys wearing Eton collars. The front row are showing off their clog-irons, that most wonderfully practical and comfortable footwear for adverse conditions, either weather or working. Looking closely at the picture, there is a mysterious marking on the right, as if a figure or figures have been painted out. The coping stones on the wall are not continuous and there are upright lines, which could be the 'remains' of trouser legs.

Back Row: Janie Thompson; Sally Byers; Cathy Green; Emily Stanard; Grace Errington; Peggy Ritson; Joyce Hope; Mary Glaister.

Middle Row: Lenora Bell; Eva Latimer; Doreen Jackson; Ella Dixon; unknown; Lily Smith; Mabel Thompson; Louise Hudson.

Front Row: Isabel Stevenson; Dorothy Carruthers; Elsie Lancaster; Norah Jobson; Gwen Armstrong; Peggy Bell; Margery Robinson; Jeannie Hill.

Back row: Mary Bell; Jeannie McGuinness; Louvain Martin; Ada Mallinson; Edith Bell; unknown; Lilian Dewhurst; Jeannie Blaylock.
Front row: Gwen Wilson; Flo Nixon; Doris Collinson; Mary Faulder; Annie Byers; Carol Watson; Doris MacDonald.

BRAMPTON COUNCIL SCHOOL, 1927

Back Row: S. Harding; N. Armstrong; M. Maughan; unknown; J. Beck; -. O'Hara; N. Armstrong.

Middle Row: -. Allison; T. Carruthers; J. Metcalfe; T. Walker; R. Smith; unknown.

Front Row: H. Evans; T. Hill; W. Edger; J. Sinclair; -. Thompson; J. Thompson; K. Park.

BRAMPTON COUNCIL SCHOOL, 1927(?)
Back Row: Mabel Winthrop; Myrtle Evans; Doris Bell; Mary Bell (twins); Annie Byers; Mary Bowes; Doris Collinson.
Second Row: Katy Robinson; Agnes Mark; Mary Fisher; Nancy Foley; Kathleen Sanderson; Eunice Latimer.
Third Row: Ada Mallinson; Maud Bone; Ivy Thompson; Ada Wannop; Ethel Wilson; Jeannie Blaylock; Bertha Hamilton; Willie Bell.
Front Row: John Noble; Walter Reay; Illtyd Thomas; Willie Rowley; Douglas Clark; William Liddell.

How quickly time passes! This picture is over fifty years old. It is the first intake into the fourth year at Irthing Valley School in 1951.

BRAMPTON JUNIOR SCHOOL, 1956, THE CENTENARY YEAR.
Back Row: Ian Thompson; Ian de Graaf; Jimmy McCullough; Maurice Thompson. Middle Row: Mr. S. A. Bell; John Graham; Derek Woodbridge; Margaret Walker; Agnes Whiteford; David Thompson; Peter Reay; Mr. Todd (Chairman of the Governors)
Front Row: Pamela Monkhouse; Jean Little; Jennifer Todd; Rosemary Ross; Eileen Barnes; Julia Strathdee; Anne Robertson; Jennifer Holland

BRAMPTON JUNIOR SCHOOL, 1956 – CENTENARY YEAR.
Back row: John Smith; -. Hodgson; Neil Graham; Kenneth Harding; Barry Twizell; Richard Bland; Peter Ridpath. (1 boys name missing)
Second Row: Mr. S. A. Bell (Headmaster); Brian Dixon; David Latimer; John Batey; Dorothy Hetherington; -. Bland(?); Ann van Limbeck; Raymond Glendinning; John Winthrop; Richard Little; Mr. Hetherington (Form teacher).
Third Row: Kathleen Harrison; Elizabeth Tate; Christine Davidson; unknown; Pamela Carnegie; Vivian Whittaker; Dorothy Carruthers; Audrey McDougall; Evelyn Scudder.
Front Row: Brian Dixon; Billy Irving; Peter Thompson; Malcolm Hunter.

The picture below is one that cannot accurately be dated. Some girls appear on it who are on other photographs, but were there two classes combined, bearing in mind the number of people who are shown?

Back Row: Margaret Sanderson; Mavis Armstrong; Jean Oliphant; Doreen Rowntree; Grace Winthrop; Annie Byers; Katy Little; Isobel Thompson; Thelma Wright; Peggy Armstrong; Edna Surtees; Doreen Barclay; Doreen Jackson; unknown; Mary Park.
Middle Row: Lizzie Robinson; Eliza Smith; Marion Hodgson; Peggy Burke; Isobel Coulthard; Betty Baker; Kitty Faulder; Violet Reay; Grace Errington; Mary Glaister; Mary Hutton; Nancy Foley; Peggy Brayton; Ella Graham.
Front Row: Margery Robinson; Joyce Hope; Olive Johnston; Jeannie Atkinson; Norah Jobson; Betty Foster; Winnie Musgrave.

I have mentioned Croft House Academy earlier in this section and also dealt with it briefly in an earlier book. Because of the kindness of a friend, I have managed to copy the first page of the prospectus, which Joseph Couthard produced. The school had a very high reputation throughout Britain. There were boys from all over the country and from overseas during the latter part of the nineteenth century, an astonishing achievement for a school in a small northern town, well away from the usually accepted location of schools of excellence.

The prospectus is quite detailed and is a little difficult to read, written as it is in an unusual Victorian script. It has also been necessary to print it sideways to enlarge the writing, as the paper size is non-standard, which means it cannot be easily accommodated on a conventional modern page.

Croft House Academy, Brampton.

Croft House Academy, near Brampton, is delightfully situated on an eminence which overlooks the great Vale of Cumberland. The Buildings have been recently erected, and are arranged so as to be conducive to the leading objects of an Educational Establishment. The air is highly salubrious - the play-ground is high, dry, and open, and the surrounding district which abounds with objects of deep interest to the Philosophic Student, is exceedingly healthy. In addition to the Proprietor, I. Coulthard, there are generally four other well-qualified and experienced Teachers with whose assistance a course of instruction is given in Classics, Mathematics, and Philosophy, which will enable a young Gentleman on leaving School to enter any of the Universities to adopt the Naval the Military or the Engineering Profession - or to devote himself to the pursuits of Commerce or Agriculture.

Lectures on Mechanics, Astronomy, Chemistry, Geology, Physiology, &c, are regularly delivered by the Masters, and also on various branches of experimental philosophy by the Senior pupils, suitable apparatus being provided for that purpose. - Proper discipline is maintained by appealing to the religious principles, reasoning powers, and moral feelings of the pupils. - fines and corporal punishments being entirely discarded as worse than useless, the Conductor having found, from an experience of 26 years, that by treating a boy as a reasonable being, it is not only possible but comparatively easy to induce upright conduct, gentlemanly demeanour, and proper deference to the rights and wishes of others. So the early formation of habits of industry and punctuality - the cultivation of a love of knowledge - the elevation of the moral feelings - and the general development of the intellectual and physical powers, - the Conductor has directed his most strenuous efforts; and the unprecedented encouragement he has received, together with the high terms of approbation expressed by those who have witnessed his public examinations, sufficiently demonstrate the excellence of his educational plans: - in proof of which reference will be given on application to parties who have had boys on the establishment, or to others who have had opportunities of personally inspecting the School.

A feature that has proved to be very popular in previous books is the copying of the pages from old directories of the town. For this edition, I have chosen two, the first from 1861 and the second from 1929, which latter will certainly revive personal memories for some townspeople.

BRAMPTON.

BRAMPTON is a market town and parish, and the capital of the barony of Gilsland, in the ward of Eskdale ; 9 miles E. by S. from Carlisle, 11 miles S. from Longtown, 22 N. from Penrith, and 1½ miles S. of the Newcastle and Carlisle Railway. The town, which is of considerable antiquity, is long and straggling, situated in a deep and narrow vale (between the rivers Irthing and Gelt), round which the country swells into considerable eminences. The wall erected by the Romans, to repress the inroads of the Picts, is two miles to the north of Brampton ; and the neighbourhood abounds with interesting remains, chiefly of Roman origin. At its eastern end is a remarkable conical hill, of considerable elevation, called the mote ; and about a mile and a half to the south, on the banks of the romantic Gelt, is a freestone rock bearing a Roman inscription, still legible. with a date as remote as the reign of the Emperor Severus. It was at a tavern in High Cross street, called the " Freemasons' Arms," that the keys of Carlisle were delivered to Prince Charles Stuart, by the mayor and aldermen of that city, in 1745 ; here the prince found a considerable quantity of arms, and his father was proclaimed king of Great Britain, and himself regent, by the magistrates. The working classes here are chiefly employed in weaving checks, ginghams, &c., for the Carlisle houses, and in spinning and weaving linen for domestic uses. The adjacent coal works, the property of the Earl of Carlisle, give employment to a large number of persons ; the railway, between Newcastle and Carlisle, passes about 1¼ miles to the south-east. The cupola of the market hall was constructed in 1817, at the expense of the Earl. The present nobleman is lord of the manor or honour, and holds a court in April and October, in an apartment over the Market-place ; and the county magistrates hold petty sessions each alternate Wednesday. Brampton is a polling station for the eastern division of the county. The parish church of Saint Martin, a neat stone structure, was repaired at considerable expense in 1827, when a tower was added to it, and a peal of good bells hung therein—the latter, together with a fine organ, were presented by the late vicar, the Rev. Thomas Ramshay. The dissenting places of worship in the town are the English Presbyterian, Independent, Wesleyan, and Primitive Methodist chapels. About two miles and a half N.E. of Brampton, beautifully situated, is Naworth Castle, the ancient baronial seat of the Lords of Gilsland, and now of the Earl of Carlisle. The apartments of Lord William Howard, remembered by the appellation of " Belted Willy," the terror of the moss troopers, in the reign of Elizabeth, are still preserved, with their ancient furniture. The market, which is on Wednesday, is well supplied with corn and provisions of all sorts, woollens, drapery, &c. ; fairs, April 20th, second Wednesday after Whitsuntide, second Wednesday in September, and October 23rd. Brampton parish contained, in 1841, 3,304 inhabitants, and, in 1851, 3,824.—EASBY township, with the hamlet of Crooked Holme, is situated 1½ miles north-north-east of Brampton, and contained a population, in 1851, of 99 souls. —NAWORTH, with the hamlet of Boothby, is a small township, containing Naworth Castle and a few scattered dwellings, situate on the south side of the river Irthing, and distant 2½ miles north-east from Brampton.

CLERGY, GENTRY, &c.

Armstrong Mr. Joseph, High Cross street
Armstrong William, Esq., Garden terrace
Atkinson Rev. (Wesleyan), Back street
Bell Mrs., Tree house
Bell Mr. John Losh, Tree house
Bennett Rev. Peter, B.A. (curate), Back street
Benson Rev. Christopher, M.A. (vicar), Unity
Carrick George Lowther, Esq., Rose villa

Carrick William, Esq., Back street
Cocks Miss Amelia, Back street
Coulthard Joseph, Esq., J.P., Croft house
Farish Mr. Isaac, Greenfield house
Fleming Miss Elizabeth, Back street
Gillbanks Miss Rebecca, Scotch road
Graham Mr. James, Front street
Graham Mr. Robert, Front street
Harding Mrs. William, Front street
Johnstone John Joseph, Esq., Back street
Latimer Mr. William, Back street
Lee John, Esq., West hill house

Maughan Mrs. Margaret, Elm cottage
Moses Bellas, Esq., Prospect house
Moses Mr. Thomas
Ramshay George, Esq., Front street
Ramshay Thomas, Esq.
Robinson Anthony, Esq., Back street
Routledge Mrs. Rachael, Front street
Scott Mr. James, Back street
Taylor Rev. Peter (Presbyterian)
Todd Mr. Edward, Front street
Waugh John George, Esq., Ridge house

TRADES AND PROFESSIONS.

[h. signifies private residence.]

Armstrong Mrs. Frances, confectioner, Front street
Armstrong Mrs. Jane, milliner, Market place
Armstrong John, grocer and provision dealer, High Cross street
Armstrong John, shopkeeper, Back street
Armstrong John, black and whitesmith, Moat side
Armstrong Mrs. Mary, shopkeeper, Market place
Armstrong Joseph, boot and shoemaker, Back street
Armstrong Thomas, linen and woollen draper, silk mercer, &c., Market place
Armstrong Thomas, carrier, Front street
Armstrong Wilfred, printer and bookbinder, Front street
Armstrong William, farmer, Tarn end
Armstrong William, surgeon, Garden terrace
Atkinson Ann, shopkeeper, Pickering's hill
Atkinson Joseph, boot and shoemaker, Back street
Barker James, "Crown Inn," Front street
Barker William, plasterer, Front street
Barnes Miss, dressmaker, Back street
Burns Peter, nurseryman, Church lane
Batey Mrs. Mabel, farmer, Moat side
Bell David, shopkeeper, Newcastle road
Bell James, skinner, Scotch road
Bell John Losh, linen and woollen draper, silk mercer, hosier, &c., Front street
Bell John, butcher, High Cross street
Bell Miss Mary, "Joiners' Arms," Market place
Bell Robert, brazier and tinman, Low Cross street
Bell Thomas, farmer, Town foot
Bell Thomas, "Ridge House Inn," Sands
Black Robert, registrar of births and deaths for the Brampton district, Front street
Blain Robert, flour dealer, Market place

Blaylock Joseph, plumber and gasfitter, Front street
Brown Tamer, "Odd Fellows' Arms"
Brown Thomas, tailor, Moat side
Brown Thomas, old clothes dealer, Back street
Burn Peter, linen and woollen draper and hosier, Front street
Cairns Ralph, watch and clockmaker and auctioneer, Back street
Carlisle John, veterinary surgeon, Back street
Carrick George, solicitor, Rose villa
Carrick and Lee, solicitors, bankers, and clerks to the Magistrates for the Haltwistle division of North, Back street
Carrick William, solicitor and coroner for the Eastern Division of the county, steward for the Earl of Carlisle's Barony of Gilsland and other manors, clerk to the Magistrates of Eskdale ward, and to the Trustees of Brampton and Longtown Turnpike Trust, clerk to the commissioners of property and income tax, and commissioner for taking oaths in Chancery (see Carrick and Lee)
Carrick William, brewer, Old brewery
Chalmers Peter, brewer and maltster, Back street
Charlton N., "Bush Inn," Back street
Cheesbrough Thomas, printer, bookbinder, stationer, newsagent, and stamp office, Back street
Clementson Edward, boot and shoemaker, Market place
Coulthard Joseph, classical and commercial school, Croft house
Crozier Ann, "Blue Bell," Front street
Cullen Joseph, "Commercial Inn," & wine and spirit merchant, Back street
Dent Mrs. Elizabeth Ann, milliner and dressmaker, Front street
Dixon Miss Margaret, grocer, Back street

Dobinson Christopher Charters (firm of Dobinson and Smith), h., Moat terrace

Dobinson and Smith, wholesale and retail grocers and tea dealers, and seedsmen, High Cross street

Dodd John, "White Lion," High Cross street

Dodd Joseph, clogger, Front street

Elliot George, wine and spirit merchant, High Cross street, h., Edenbank, Wetheral

Elliot Robert, boot and shoemaker, Back street

Elliott Robert, shoemaker, Moat side

Elliott Mrs. Sarah, straw bonnet maker, Moat side

Farish Isaac, linen and woollen draper, High Cross street, h., Greenfield house

Fleming Miss Mary, grocer, High Cross street

Forster Thomas, solicitor, and agent to the Globe Fire and Life Insurance Co., Back street, h., North view

Foster Edward, tailor, Front street

Fowler John Thomas, superintendent of police constabulary, Station

Gaddes Mrs. Mary, shopkeeper, Back street

Gash John, cooper, Back street

Gash Simpson, cooper, Back street

Gill Margaret, shopkeeper, Back street

Graham James (firm of Moses and Graham)

Graham John, farmer, Aaron's town

Graham Joseph, "George Inn" and posting house, Market place

Graham Robert, linen and woollen draper, silk mercer, &c., High Cross street, h., Front street

Hall Mrs. Margaret, straw bonnet maker, Market place

Halliburton John, tallow chandler and grocer, Front street

Hamilton Mrs. Elizabeth, straw bonnet maker, High Cross street

Hamilton James, nail manufacturer, Cross street

Hardy John, marine store dealer, Front street

Hardy William, boot and shoemaker, Back street

Harrison George, earthenware and marine store dealer, Front street

Harrison Thomas, grocer and provision dealer, Front street

Haugh Thomas, grocer and druggist, Back street

Hetherington George, ironmonger, Low Cross street

Hetherington John, wine and spirit merchant, and farmer, Front street

Hetherington John, "Scotch Arms," Back street

Hetherington Robert, butcher, Front street

Hewett George, tailor, Front street

Hodgson Mrs. Mary, printer, bookseller, binder, stationer, and dealer in paper hangings, Back street

Holmes William, banker's clerk, Back street

Hope Miss Elizabeth, "Crown and Anchor Inn," Front street

Hudspith John, "Howard Arms," posting house, and farmer, Front street

Humble Mrs. Margaret, milliner and straw bonnet maker, Market place

Humble William, joiner and cabinet maker, Market place

Irving Joseph, cartwright and joiner, Moat side

Irving Robert, shoeing smith, Front street

Irving William, black and whitesmith, and agricultural implement maker, Back street

Jameison Robert, grocer, Chapel street

James Mrs. Sarah, dressmaker, Moat side

Jefferson Jacob, shoemaker, Loning

Johnson Andrew, painter, Market place

Johnstone John Joseph, surgeon, Back street

Knott Mrs. Sarah, "Sandhouse Inn," the Sands

Latimer Robert, printer, bookbinder, bookseller, and newsagent, Front street

Law Mary and Elizabeth, "Temperance Hotel," High Cross street

Lawson Miss Margaret, grocer and game dealer, Market place

Lear Thos., painter, Market place

Lee John (firm of Carrick and Lee), solicitor, clerk to the land and assessed tax commissioners, and registrar of the County court, Back street, h., West hill

Leighton William, slater, Back street

Little George, butcher, Low Cross street

Makepeace John, master of Union Work-house

Mark Bell, butcher, Back street

Martin Mrs. Barbara, glass & earthenware dealer, High Cross street

Milburn Mrs. Elizabeth, furnishing and general ironmonger, High Cross street

Milburn William, agent for bone manures and sheep and cattle dressings, High Cross street

Mitchenson Thomas, "Barley Stack Inn," Newcastle road

Modlen George, hat and cap manufacturer, Front street

Moses Bellas, surgeon, Prospect house

Moses and Graham, iron, timber, and slate merchants, furnishing ironmongers, bacon curers, &c., Back street

Moses Joseph (firm of Moses and Graham)

Moses Thomas, linen and woollen draper, Market place, h., Oak wood

Mounsey William, "Red Lion," Front street

Nairn Miss, Boarding school, Wetheral
Nichol Adam, cooper, Pickering's hill
Nixon James, grocer and tea dealer, Front street
Nixon Walter, hairdresser, Back street
Noble John, joiner and cabinet maker, Back street
Oliver John, "Black Bull," Front street
Orwin Miss Anne, milliner and straw bonnet maker, Market place
Palmer David, farmer, Park barn
Palmer William, farmer, Hembles gate
Park George, grocer, High Cross street
Parker Mrs. Isabella, farmer, Aaron's town
Parker John and Robert, linen and woollen drapers, Front street
Parker Joseph, joiner, Back street
Parker Joseph, tallow chandler, Back street
Parker Mrs. Mary, "Wheat Sheaf," Back street
Parker Robert, tea dealer and grocer, Market place
Parker Thomas, farmer, Gelt bridge
Pears John, druggist and grocer, Market place
Pearson William, beer retailer, Front street
Penfold Henry, painter and glazier, Front street
Phillips Joseph, watch and clockmaker, High Cross street
Phillips Mrs. Mary, shoe dealer, Market place
Pickering John, tea agent, Back street
Ramshay George, solicitor, clerk to Guardians, and superintendent registrar of Brampton Union, Back street, h., Front street
Ramshay and Latimer, solicitors
Reay James, "Nag's Head," Market place
Reed Miss Ann, grocer, Market place
Reed John, saddler and harness maker, Back street
Reed Jonathan, watch and clockmaker, Market place
Richardson William, "Shoulder of Mutton," Front street
Richardson William, clock and watchmaker and cabinet maker, Market place
Riddle Mrs. Janet, farmer, Brampton fell
Ridley John, skinner, Town foot
Ridley William, shopkeeper, Town foot
Robinson John Clement, yeoman, Back street
Routledge Mrs. Hannah, eating house, Market place
Routledge Joseph, "Sportsman Inn," and mason, Front street
Routledge Miss Margaret, glass and earthenware dealer, Market place
Routledge Thomas, tanner and currier, Front street
Rowntree William, grocer and flour dealer, Moat side

Rowntree William, grocer, tea dealer, and seedsman, Cross street
Rutherford George, clog and last maker, Moat side
Rutherford Miss Harriet, milliner, Moat side
Rutherford James, grocer, Back street
Salkeld John, tailor, Cross street
Salkeld Mrs. Sarah, straw bonnet maker, High cross street
Scott Robert, dyer, Front street
Sewell Mrs. Elizabeth, infant schoolmistress, Back street
Slater Miss Sarah, shopkeeper, Front street
Sloan Robert, shoemaker, Back street
Sloan William, boot and shoemaker, Front street
Smith Thomas (firm of Dobinson & Smith), h. Moat terrace
Snowball Cuthbert, wholesale and retail wine and spirit merchant, tea and coffee dealer, "Old King's Arms," Back street (see advertisement)
Stephenson Samuel, "Earl Grey Inn," Sands
Swallow Mrs. Sarah, "Freemason's Arms," Cross street
Taylor Christopher, druggist and grocer, Back street
Taylor Henry, "Shepherd Inn," Front street
Taylor Mrs. Margaret, "String of Horses," Back street
Thompson Dinah, "Half Moon," Front street
Thompson James, clock maker, Back street
Thompson John, grocer, Front street
Thompson John, farmer, Wreay
Thompson Maria and Sons, coal and lime proprietors (Jas. Parker, agent). Staithes
Thompson Thomas, hair dresser, Front street
Tinling Mrs. Margaret, dressmaker, Back street
Tinling Thomas, shoemaker, Back street
Tinniswood Elizabeth, shopkeeper, Front street
Todd Edward, joiner, builder, cabinet maker, and furniture broker, Moat side
Topping John, tailor, Market place
Topping M. A., milliner, Back street
Townley Elizabeth, lodgings, Chapel street
Walker James, parish clerk, Town foot
Walker Miss Jane, dressmaker, Town foot
Wallace Richard, tailor, String of horses lane
Wallace William, joiner and cartwright, Scotch road
Wannop Arthur, saddler & harness maker, Back street
Wannop Arthur Johnson, draper, Front street
Wannop Charles, linen and woollen draper, silk mercer, Market place, h., Moat terrace

Ward Mrs. Margaret, "Coach and Horses Inn," Back street
Watson James, "Sampson Inn," and wine and spirit merchant, Front street
Welsh James, painter, Back street
Westmoreland Thomas, "Globe Inn" and posting house, Market place
Wilkinson Joseph, tailor, Back street
Wilson Miss, Ladies' seminary
Winterop Margaret, dressmaker, Back street
Younger Thomas, chemist and druggist, Market place

EASBY.

Trades and Professions.

Bell William, farmer, Old church
Boustead Thomas, farmer
Bowman James, farmer, Brec'. on hill
Dodd John, farmer, Crookedholme
Hetherington James, "Johnson's Arms," Cambeck bridge
Routledge Mrs. farmer, Ridge side
Simpson John, farmer, Crookedholme
Smith John, farmer, Coathill
Wallace William, farmer

NAWORTH.

Gentry.

Carlisle Right Hon. Earl of, Naworth castle
Horncastle W. W., Esq., Boothby

Trades and Professions.

Blain Robert, miller and farmer, New mills
Dobson William, farmer, Tarn houses
Halliburton and Gill, farmers, Warren house
Heward Hugh, "Lanercost Inn"
Grisdale John, gamekeeper to the Right Hon. Earl of Carlisle
Hetherington John, farmer, Milton hill
Hodgson James, farmer, Denton mill
Irving John, blacksmith and agricultural implement maker, Abbey bridge end
Jackson Joseph, farmer, Beck gate
Ramshay John, steward to the Right Hon. Earl of Carlisle, Barns
Richardson William, farmer, Cumcatch
Routledge John, miller, Bridge end
Thirlwall Mrs., farmer, Boothby
Wannop Charles, miller and farmer, Denton mill

INFORMATION OF PUBLIC MEN AND INSTITUTIONS CONNECTED WITH THE TOWN.

Post Office.

Back street.

Joseph Coulthard, postmaster. Letters dispatched to Haltwhistle, Haydonbridge and Hexham at 7.30 a.m.; Carlisle, Hexham, Newcastle-on-Tyne, and Gateshead, 2.30 p.m.; Carlisle, 6.30 p.m. Arrive from Carlisle, 8.30 a.m.; Hexham, Newcastle-on-Tyne, and Gateshead at 9.26 a.m.; Haltwhistle, Haydonbridge, and Hexham, at 4.30 p.m. On Sundays, dispatched to Hexham, Newcastle-on-Tyne, and Gateshead, at 5.15 p.m.; Carlisle, at 7.11 p.m.; arrive from Carlisle at 8.20 a.m.; Hexham, Newcastle-on-Tyne, and Gatehead, at 10.30 a.m.
Letters to and from Bewcastle, Monday, Wednesday, and Friday, at 10 a.m.; Tuesday, Thursday, and Saturday at 2 p.m.

Bankers.

Brampton Bank,

Carrick and Lee, proprietors
Draw on Glyn and Co., London.

Brampton Savings Bank

(branch of the Carlisle Savings Bank, established 1818),
W. P. Johnson, and } sub-treasurers
Rev. C. Benson,
Thomas Cheesbrough, clerk

Public Establishments.

Gasworks,
Town foot.

Stamp Office,
Thomas Cheesbrough, sub-distributor

Brampton Mechanics' Institute,
Joseph Coulthard, president
John Graham, and } vice-presidents
John Bell,
Thomas Moses, treasurer
Thomas Cheesbrough, sec. and librarian

Odd Fellows' Lodge (Royal Brampton),
Held at the White Lion, 240 members

Loyal Tradesmen's Pride Lodge,
Held at the Bush Inn, 75 members

Brampton Benefit Building Society,
Carrick and Lee, solicitors
Thomas Cheesbrough, secretary

Talkin Tarn Amateur Regatta and Wrestling Society,
Thomas Cheesbrough, secretary

Brampton Union Workhouse,
George Ramshay, clerk to board
John Makepeace, master
Mrs. Makepeace, matron
John Graham, M.D., medical officer
William Armstrong, assistant ditto
John Routledge, relieving officer

County Court,
Howard Arms,
Theophilus Hastings Ingham, Esq., judge
Mr. John Lee, registrar
Wm. Holmes, registrar's clerk
Wm. Browne, high bailiff
John Hogg, assistant bailiff

Inland Revenue Office,
White Lion Inn.

Constabulary Station,
Newcastle road.
John Thomas Fowler, superintendent
William Smith, serjeant

Public Officers :—

Relieving Officer and Registrar of Marriages for Union, and Registrar of Births and Deaths for Brampton District,
Robert Black

Registrar of Births and Deaths for Hayton District,
Ralph Watson

Registrar of Births and Deaths for Walton District,
Isaac Dalton

Public Vaccinator,
John Joseph Johnstone

Magistrates,
Wm. Ponsonby Johnson, James Fawcett, Joseph Dacre, Wm. Henry Ewart, Joseph Coulthard, Thos. Henry Graham, Philip Henry Howard, Esqs., and Rev. Isaac Dodgson

Places of Worship.
St. Martin's Church,
Rev. Christopher Benson, M.A., vicar
Rev. Peter Bennett, B.A., curate

English Presbyterian Chapel,
Rev. Peter Taylor, minister

Independent Chapel,
Ministers various

Wesleyan Chapel,
Ministers various

Primitive Chapel,
Ministers various

Public Schools.
National,
Wm. Hugill, master
Miss Fowler, mistress

Presbyterian,
Irving Steele, master

Infant,
Mrs. Elizabeth Hayden, mistress

Carriers to

Carlisle—Carruthers and Armstrong, every day, except Wednesdays and Sundays

Alston—Greaves, from " King's Arms," Wednesday

Renwick—Walton, from " Joiners' Arms," Wednesday

The **KELLY'S 1929 DIRECTORY** entry starts, very considerately, at the bottom of a page!

BRAMPTON is a small market town, township and parish, and the head of a union and county court district, with a station on the Newcastle and Carlisle section of the London and North Eastern railway, 11 miles east-north-east from Carlisle, 47½ west from Newcastle-on-Tyne and 303 from London. It is in the Northern division of the county, Eskdale ward and petty sessional division, rural deanery of Brampton and archdeaconry and diocese of Carlisle. The town is attractively situated in a deep and narrow valley between the rivers Gelt and Irthing, and on the road from Carlisle to Haltwhistle, and is about 2½ miles from the confluence of these streams, and 2 miles south of the Roman wall; it consists of two principal streets and a spacious market place; the houses, for the most part, are irregularly built, but many have now been rebuilt, and the place has generally a neat appearance: the town is lighted with gas from works belonging to a company formed in

CUMBERLAND.

1836, and is supplied with excellent water obtained from the glacier spring at Farlam and from the Geltsdale waterworks by agreement with the Carlisle Corporation: there is also a complete system of sewerage, carried out at a cost of £4,000. The ancient parish church of St. Martin, appropriated by Robert de Vaux to Lanercost Abbey soon after 1169, was pulled down, with the exception of the chancel, in 1788; this portion, now in use only as a mortuary chapel, stands on an eminence about 1½ miles north-west, overlooking the valley of the Irthing, and is a building of stone, with some Norman features, a porch, and a turret containing one bell, cast by Mears during the last century: the piscina and an aumbry remain, and there are several inscribed floor stones: on the south wall of the porch is a stone discovered in 1842 by the late Mr. Robert Bell, of The Nook, Irthington, and inscribed to Richard de Caldecote, vicar here, ob. 1346, and on the same wall is another stone, with inscription to Richard Culcheth, vicar, 1702, with a rhyming epitaph of six lines; on the north wall of the porch is fixed the side slab of a panelled altar tomb, disinterred from the churchyard in 1858, and displaying within quatrefoils three shields of arms:—1st, a bend chequy, for Vaux of Triermain; 2nd, three escallops, 2 and 1, for Dacre of Naworth; and 3rd, a cross fleury, with an escallop in the dexter chief, for Delamore: in the exterior south wall of the chapel is a segmental arch covering an ancient tombstone, which bears an incised cross of graceful character; on the south side of the churchyard lies another stone, carved with a cross and sword and the letters A. M. below the arms of the cross: at the base of the north slope of the churchyard are remains of Roman masonry, forming a considerable block, and near this is the obliterated site of St. Ninian's or the Priest's well; some other portions of Roman work have been met with in the ground added to the churchyard in 1858, and a Roman amphora was dug up by the sexton in 1886: the churchyard was further enlarged by one acre in 1861, and in 1890 nearly two acres more were added; it now covers an area of somewhat less than four acres, and serves as a public cemetery.

On the removal of the greater part of the old church in 1788, the materials were used in enlarging the hospital chapel, which, together with four of the almshouses, were reconstructed to serve as a parish church on the site of the present church of St. Martin; this church was consecrated by Bishop Douglas in the same year: it was considerably enlarged in 1827-8, at a cost of £1,800, when a peal of 6 bells was hung, 4 of these, besides the organ, being the gift of the Rev. Thomas Ramshay, then vicar.

The present church of St. Martin, erected in 1877-8, at a cost of £8,643, occupies the site of the former structure, and is a building of red sandstone from the Gelt quarries, in the Transitional Early English style, from designs by Mr. Philip Webb, architect, of London, and consists of chancel, nave of four bays, aisles, vestry of two stages at the end of the north aisle, north porch, and a western tower, completed in 1906, and containing the 6 bells from the previous church, and a clock with chimes and three dials, the total cost amounting to £2,250; the lower portion of the tower forms a porch and baptistery: the chancel is separated from the nave by a low stone screen: the stained east window was erected by subscription in 1881 as a memorial to the Hon. Charles Wentworth George Howard M.P. d. 11 April, 1879; there are also numerous other stained windows, all of which were designed by Sir E. Burne Jones bart. A.R.A. some being memorials: there is a tablet, with bust, to the Rev. Thomas Ramshay B.C.L. vicar here, d. 20 Dec. 1840, and Maria, his widow, d. 3 Nov. 1846; two windows, a tablet containing 60 names, and a soldiers' chapel with accommodation for 40 people, were erected to the men who fell in the Great War, 1914-18: and in the baptistery are other tablets, two of which bear the names of the vicars of Brampton: the communion plate includes two flagons, a silver chalice (called the Newcastle chalice), paten, alms dish and three plates, and is mostly of the 17th century, the chalice being rather earlier: there are 500 sittings. The register dates from the year 1663; average tithe rent charge, £50. The living is a vicarage, net yearly value £400, without residence, in the gift of Lady Cecilia Roberts, and held since 1926 by the Rev. Edwin Thomas Shepherd B.A. of the Royal University of Ireland, and surrogate. The Presbyterian congregation here dates from 1662, in which year the Rev. Nathaniel Burnand, then vicar of Brampton, was ejected from the living, and 10 years after was licensed as a Presbyterian minister. The church, built in 1854, at a cost of £1,100, £800 of

which was contributed by Mr. Barbour, of Manchester, is a structure in the Gothic style. There are also Primitive Methodist, Wesleyan Methodist and Roman Catholic chapels. The Moot Hall, which stands in the centre of the market place, was erected by Frederick, 5th Earl of Carlisle, in 1817, on the site of a former building, and is an octagonal edifice of stone, with a cupola containing a clock; the lower portion, which forms a piazza, has lately been enclosed, and is used on market days for the sale of butter and eggs; above this is a spacious hall, the entrance to which is approached by two flights of stone steps. On the west side of the Moot Hall still remain the old iron stocks, and on the same side is the bull ring. In 1904 a monument was erected at Capon Tree, on the site of a tree of that name, in memory of six gentlemen adherents of Prince Charles, the Young Pretender, who were hanged here Oct. 11th, 1746; the monument stands in a small plantation on the road which leads to Gelt woods. At the west end of the town is a large granite monument with a bronze sunk medallion, erected in memory of George John Johnson esq. of Castlesteads, who died in 1896, and was connected with Brampton for very many years. The magistrates' office and police station form a building of red sandstone, erected in 1856, on the site of the old National School; the petty sessions are held here every alternate Wednesday. St. Martin's Hall, in Front street, erected, at a cost of £5,000, as a memorial to the late Lt.-Col. Thompson, of Milton Hall, consists of a large hall capable of seating 500 persons, a library, kitchen, dressing rooms &c. the whole being attached to the Church of England in perpetuity. A Masonic and an Oddfellows' Lodge are maintained here. The market is held on Wednesday, in the spacious market place. Fairs for sheep and cattle are held on April 20th, the second Wednesday after Whitsuntide, the second Wednesday in September and the third Friday in October. Hiring and pleasure fairs are held on Whit Wednesday and on the first Wednesday after the 11th of November. The principal hotel is the White Lion. The Tweed mill, burnt down in 1874, and since rebuilt, is the property of Lady Dorothy G. Henley, and is used as a public hall, but a part has been converted into a wool store. The Central Hall, in Main street, will seat 300 persons. The Brampton Agricultural Society was formed in 1854, and numbers about 200 members; the society holds an annual show of live stock &c. in September. Talkin Tarn Amateur Rowing Club was formed in 1854, and numbers about 500 members, under the presidency of the Hon. Geoffrey William A. Howard. The head quarters of the club are at Talkin Tarn, where there is an excellent boat-house, a bathing-house and nearly forty racing and pleasure boats. A regatta is held annually. The club season opens on Easter Monday in each year. There is also an Angling Association. The Total Abstinence Society, formed in 1882, numbers about 300 members. In 1891 a scheme of allotments was carried out, and 4½ acres of land, situated south-west of the town, appropriated for the purpose; an addition of 6½ acres of land, near the Carlisle road, has since been made. It is controlled by the Garden Allotments Committee and Small Holdings Association.

Talkin Tarn, a lake covering an area of 64½ acres, is pleasantly situated 2 miles south of the town, and in the parish of Brampton. The banks on the north and east are covered with thriving plantations, and the lake is well stocked with fish. There is a boat-house, a bathing-house and a temperance hotel. East of the town is a conical hill, called the "Mote," 360 feet high, surrounded by a fosse, and thickly overgrown with trees. On the summit, which affords a very extensive view of the surrounding country, is a bronze statue of George, 7th Earl of Carlisle, erected in 1870, and designed by the late J. H. Foley esq. R.A.; on the pedestal of white sandstone is the following inscription :—"Erected by the people of Cumberland to commemorate the public service and personal worth of George William Frederick Howard, seventh Earl of Carlisle K.G.; born April 18, 1802, died December 5th, 1864." On the north bank of the river Gelt, 2 miles south-west of Brampton, is a rock called "The Written Rock," on which are the remains of an inscription, only a few words of which can now be made out with the naked eye. The inscription, cut by the 2nd Augustan legion, stationed here, under Agricola, the proprætor, A.D. 207, is doubtful, but appears to signify that the Vexillarii of the second legion, under Agricola, the "optio" (adjutant), were here employed in hewing stone.

BRAMPTON.   CUMBERLAND.

About a quarter of a mile south-east of Brampton old church, and a mile and a quarter south of the wall, is the site of a Roman camp or station, connected with that at Walton House (Castlesteads) by a military road; the area of the station is about 1½ acres, but its outlines are now only distinguishable by a few slightly elevated portions of the ramparts; the interior is bestrewn with débris, and within it Roman pottery and coins have often been met with. In a field on the south side, now farmed by Mr. Joseph Jefferson, are several barrows. Mr. H. McLauchlan, in 1857, fixed on it as the "Amboglanna" of the "Notitia;" but the late Rev. John Maughan, in 1870, preferred to regard it as "Congavata." In 1826 a large earthen jar was turned up here by the plough, and found to contain no fewer than 5,000 coins, all of the later empire. The bronze matrix of the common seal of Penrith was found at Brampton about 1824, having been carried away, as is supposed, during an incursion of the Scots; it is now in the possession of the Town Commissioners of Penrith. In Sept. 1903, during the progress of some excavations for a drain at the back of the then Half Moon inn, a stone axe-hammer, about 10 inches long and nearly 5 in width was found, and is now in the possession of Miss Richardson. In November, 1715, a large force under the command of Mr. Forster, who had received a general's commission from Prince James Edward Stuart, entered the town, where they proclaimed the Pretender, and hence marched to Penrith; during the rebellion of 1745, Prince Charles Edward Stuart led his troops hither to observe the movements of General Wade, who was erroneously reported to be marching from Newcastle to the relief of Carlisle; after remaining here for a week at a house in High Cross street, in which is still pointed out his council chamber, he proceeded to Carlisle, which had previously surrendered; the keys of the city were presented to the Prince at Brampton by the mayor and corporation on their knees. Among the distinguished persons born here may be mentioned James Wallace esq. who, by his talents and industry, raised himself from very humble circumstances to the office of Attorney-General, which he held in 1780, and again in 1783, but died at the age of 53 in the height of his reputation, and "when the highest honours his profession could offer or his country bestow were within his grasp." Dr. Guy Carleton, also a native of this parish, was Bishop of Bristol 1671-8, and of Chichester 1678-85, and died in 1685, after suffering much for his loyalty previous to the Restoration. The Earl of Carlisle and the trustees of the late Rosalind Countess of Carlisle are the principal landowners. Col. Charles Howard, of Naworth, who was highly instrumental in the restoration of King Charles II. was created, 30 April, 1661, "Baron Dacre of Gilsland, Viscount Howard of Morpeth and Earl of Carlisle," and subsequently went as an ambassador to Russia. Between the years 1702 and 1731, Charles Howard, 3rd Earl of Carlisle, built the splendid mansion of Castle Howard, near Malton, in Yorkshire. The area of the township is 6,134 acres of land and 132 of water. The population in 1921 was 2,590 (including inmates and officials in the Poor Law Institution), including Easby and Naworth, and of the ecclesiastical parish, 2,711.

EASBY and Crooked Holme are hamlets, and contain a few scattered houses. At Cambeck is a stone bridge of two arches, built in 1847, at a cost of about £2,000. Lady Cecilia Roberts and the trustees of the late F. P. Johnson esq. are the principal landowners.

Easby is the smallest of the three hamlets that compose the parish of Brampton, but in bygone days was a place of some importance, evidences of which are still to be found. The hamlet is intersected by many ancient roads.

NAWORTH, 1½ miles north-east, is a small hamlet, containing Naworth Castle and a few dispersed dwellings, on the south side of the river Irthing, with a station on the London and North Eastern railway, 2½ miles north-east from Brampton and 12 east from Carlisle. Naworth Castle, the seat of the Earl of Carlisle, is the chief mansion house of the great barony of Gilsland, originally at Irthington; but this distinction appears to have been transferred to Naworth in 1335, when Ranulph de Dacre, 2nd Baron Dacre, who had acquired possession of the barony by his marriage with Margaret, heiress of the Multons, obtained license from Edward III. to crenellate or fortify the mansion of Naworth. The castle is situated 2¼ miles north-east of the town of Brampton, and half a mile from Naworth station, and occupies the summit of a rocky height, rising above a deep and thickly-wooded ravine, through which two rivulets, one on the north and the other on the south, flow north-west, and join the Irthing outside the boundary of the park. The buildings surround an open courtyard, which, owing to the oblique position of the northern range, is unequal in its dimensions, the sides varying from about 106 to 140 feet; the principal front, facing the south-east, is about 256 feet in length, and two storeys in height, with an embattled parapet and square windows of two lights, chiefly on the upper floor; at either end are massive and lofty embattlemented towers with turrets, rising high above the trees, which, from a distance, conceal the main part of the fortress. The south-west, or old tower, called also the "Dacre" tower, dates in part from the 10th century; and it appears to have been the original peel tower from which the castle gradually assumed its present extent; it is 29 feet square, with walls about 7 feet thick, enclosing staircases to the various floors; in the lower stage are dungeons with ribbed vaulting, and above a guard room; the embattled parapet displays the arms of the Dacres, having been rebuilt by Sir Thomas Dacre, 9th Lord Dacre of Gillesland, in the reign of Henry VIII.; the north-east, or Lord William Howard's tower, perhaps also rebuilt by the same baron, is a work of very singular construction, owing to the acute angle formed by the walls at this point, which is spanned on the ground floor of the tower by a succession of boldly-ribbed cross arches, carrying the vault on which the upper floors are built; on the northern front this tower has been strengthened by a huge buttress, from which an arch has been thrown to the angle of the wall, giving the appearance of a blocked gateway, and supporting the upper storeys which are carried over it; these comprise the upper and lower "Glen" rooms and Lord William's bedroom, dressing-room, library and oratory, approached by a well staircase; the bedroom is panelled in oak, and over the fireplace are three shields of arms and the Dacre motto; the first floor of the block between the towers includes at one end the library, which rises through both floors, and has two large windows at the opposite end of the drawing-room, with a fine window of six lights; the top floor is occupied by the upper part of the library and more bedrooms. This block, which is two storeys in height, now consists of bedrooms, with a smoking-room at the west end on the ground floor. The first floor is occupied by the drawing and music rooms and library; above these and facing the courtyard are more bedrooms, and on the same floor facing south is the picture gallery, which runs the whole length of the block from Lord William's tower to the Dacre tower. Lord William Howard's library has the original book presses, now containing about 300 volumes. The fine oak ceiling, destroyed by fire in 1844, was elaborately carved with bold heraldic bosses, the panels between being filled with richly wrought tracery. This oak ceiling is supposed to have been brought from Kirkoswald. The oratory, which is on the same floor, contains the original altar, and is ornamented with several alabaster figures. Facing the altar is a curious painting on panel, representing the "Crucifixion," "Burial," and "Scourging" of Christ, and is dated 1514. There also is a small painted window. To the left of the altar is an entrance to a secret chamber, enclosed between the level of the oratory and the floor below. The drawing-room, entered from the hall, faces the courtyard; the walls, painted white, are hung with portraits of Thomas, 3rd Duke of Norfolk, b. 1474, d. 1554; Charles, 1st Earl of Carlisle; Ann, Countess of Pembroke; Thomas Howard, Earl of Arundel; Henry, Earl of Northampton; Thomas Howard, Earl of Suffolk; Lord Falkland; Philip Howard, brother of the 1st Earl of Carlisle, slain at Rowton Heath in 1645; Sir George Lisle, shot by the Roundheads at Colchester, 28 August, 1648; and the Hon. Charles Wentworth Howard. The music-room, entered from the drawing-room, has its walls panelled in oak and a floor of polished oak; it contains several oil paintings, including portraits of Henry VIII. and Queen Mary. The library, formerly a chapel, and next in order to the music-room, is beautifully decorated with carved oak panelling and hung with tapestry, and has a small gallery at each end. The room is lighted by windows of four and five lights; above the fireplace is a relief in gesso-duro by the late Sir Edward Burne Jones bart. and the late Sir Edgar Boehm R.A. representing a charge of a troop of horse at the battle of Flodden Field. The picture gallery is approached by an oak staircase leading from the library, as well as from the Dacre tower and Lord William's tower; it occupies the

114

side facing the south-east, overlooking the gardens, and the bedrooms on the same floor, which face the courtyard, are entered from this gallery, which is 130 feet in length and has a block oak flooring, and is panelled with oak; on its walls hang several paintings of Scripture subjects; in the hall are preserved three peculiarly carved oak figures, standing 3 feet high, which Lord William Howard (Belted Will) used to place upon the towers to represent soldiers. The north-east of the quadrangle, reached by stairs on the outside, comprises the great hall, about 100 feet in length by 27 wide, which has a fine open timber roof, constructed from designs by Mr. A. Salvin, architect, and supported on corbels, enriched with shields of arms; the walls are adorned with tapestry and armour, one suit of which is said to have been worn by "Belted Will," and hung with portraits of various royal and historic personages and others; these include full-length figures of Charles I. and his queen, Lord William Howard and Lady Elizabeth Dacre, his wife, Queen Elizabeth, Queen Catherine Parr, Philip, Earl of Arundel, and Theophilus, 2nd Earl of Suffolk; the hall is lighted at the dais end by a large oriel window of six lights, and in the upper part is a series of nine windows looking towards the courtyard; here also is hung a picture of a "Mosstrooper," by J. W. Glasse, 1854; and elsewhere on the walls are portraits of the 11th Earl of Northumberland, Oliver Cromwell, General Monk, Duke of Albemarle and Lady Mary Howard, daughter of the 1st Earl of Carlisle. The fireplace is about 15 feet wide, with a seat at each end. On each side of the fireplace, and at the north end of the hall, are carved heraldic figures of a red bull, a dolphin, a gryphon, and a sheep, or deer, bearing shields of arms of the Dacre and Greystoke families. Annexed to the hall, on the exterior front, is the Morpeth tower, built in 1845; this tower contains the "Glen room," used as a sitting-room and library, and over it are bedrooms. On the north-west side of the courtyard are the kitchen, store

room, servants' rooms and offices, contained in a block of buildings three storeys in height, and returned for some distance on the south-west side; on the parapet is a clock dial within a lozenge-shaped frame. The south-west side is partly occupied by the servants' living-rooms, and leading from the Dacre tower is a parapet walk which conducts to a small room, used as a Guard Room. On this side, near the Dacre tower, is a massive oak gate 20 feet high, with an arch rising 25 feet within a wall 7 feet thick. On the south front of the castle is a terrace, narrowing in width from 80 feet at its eastern end to less than 50 at the south angle. On this terrace stands a detached tower, about 36 by 30 feet, and anciently called the "bote," or fuel house; it was built by Thomas, Lord Dacre, and bears the initials of himself and his wife, and the escallop of that family. At the north-west corner is the Stanley tower, built in 1881, and containing bedrooms. More to the south are the remains of the gatehouse, displaying on the front the arms of the Howards and Dacres. On the 18th May, 1844, shortly after 5 p.m. a disastrous fire broke out in the castle, near the great hall, originating, it is said, in a flue by the porter's lodge; in spite of the most strenuous exertions, it soon spread through the whole of the buildings surrounding the courtyard, and by 8 o'clock the whole castle, except Lord William's tower and the steward's residence on the west side, was destroyed, nothing being left but the bare walls; in this terrible conflagration, much armour and some magnificent tapestry, as well as the fine oak ceiling of the hall and wainscoting brought here from Kirkoswald Castle, utterly perished: but some of the valuable objects of antiquity, books and panel pictures were fortunately saved. The castle was restored and refitted during the period 1844-5 by George, 6th Earl of Carlisle K.G. under the direction of Mr. Anthony Salvin, architect. The west park extends over 287 acres, and the east park 175 acres.

OFFICIAL ESTABLISHMENTS, LOCAL INSTITUTIONS &c.

Post, M. O., T. & T. E. D. Office, Front street. Letters should have Cumberland added

COUNTY MAGISTRATES FOR THE ESKDALE PETTY SESSIONAL DIVISION.

For addresses of magistrates see complete list at Front of Book.

Addison John J	Graham Thos. Hy. Boileau
Arnott James M.D	Halifax F. J
Carlisle Earl of	Hodgson George
Dobson William	Jackson Hugh
Dodd G	MacInnes Miss D
Ferguson T. H	Roberts Charles Henry
Graham Robert Gibbons	Routledge George Bell

The Chairman, for the time being, of the Brampton Rural District Council is an ex-officio magistrate
Clerk to the Magistrates, Henry Studholme Cartmell, Main street
Petty Sessions are held at the Magistrates' Office every alternate wednesday at 11 a.m
The following places are included in the petty sessional division:—Askerton, Brampton, Burtholme, Carlatton, Castle Carrock, Denton Nether, Denton Upper, Farlam, Irthington, Lanercost, Kingwater, Talkin, Walton High, Walton Low, Waterhead, Midgeholme, Little Corby, Cumrew, Cumwhitton, Fenton & Faugh, Hayton, Geltsdale & Northsceugh

BRAMPTON RURAL DISTRICT COUNCIL.

The parishes in the District are the same as in the Union.
Council meets at Guardians' Board room on last wednesday in each month, at 1.30 p.m.
Chairman, Charles Henry Roberts J.P. Boothby, Carlisle

Officials.

Clerk, John Gorton, 7 Victoria place, Carlisle
Treasurer, Henry Hetherington, Midland Bank Ltd. Brampton
Medical Officer of Health, James Arnott M.D., B.S., J.P. Rose villa
Surveyor of Buildings & Highways & Sanitary Inspector, George Andrew Gray, Main street, Brampton

PUBLIC ESTABLISHMENTS.

Central Hall, Main street, W. G. Harrison, sec
County Court, Magistrates' Office, His Honor Eustace Gilbert Hills K.C. judge; H. Studholme Cartmell, registrar & acting high bailiff. The County Court is

held every alternate month at the magistrates' office. The following parishes & townships are under the jurisdiction of the court:—Brampton, Castle Carrock, Cumrew, Cumwhitton, Denton Upper, Denton Nether, Farlam, Hayton, Irthington, Lanercost, Walton, Bewcastle, Stapleton, Scaleby, Hethersgill & Kirklinton Middle
For bankruptcy purposes this court is included in Carlisle district, T. B. Harston, 18 Bank street, Carlisle, official receiver
Police Station
Fire Brigade
Moot Hall, Market place
St. Martin's Hall, Front street

TERRITORIAL ARMY.

4th (Cumberland & Westmorland) Battalion, The Border Regiment (Lt. S. J. Lockyer M.C. company comdr.; Sergt. Ireland, instructor)

BRAMPTON UNION.

The Board meets at Board room on the last wednesday in each month, at 1.30 p.m.
For list of places in the union see information at the Front of Book.
The area of the union is 97,697 acres; the population in 1921 was 8,876
Chairman, Charles Henry Roberts J.P. Boothby, Carlisle
Vice-Chairman, L. Low, Green Bank, Laversdale
Clerk to the Guardians, John Gorton, Union offices, Brampton
Treasurer, Henry Hetherington, Midland Bank Ltd. Brampton
Medical Officer & Public Vaccinator, James Arnott M.D., B.S.Durh., J.P. Rose villa, Brampton
Relieving & Vaccination Officer, James Dodd, Union offices, Union lane, Brampton
The Poor Law Institution, on the east side of the town, was erected in 1875, & will hold 200 inmates; John William Dawson, master; James Arnott M.D., B.S. Durh., J.P. medical officer, Rose villa, Brampton

BRAMPTON REGISTRATION DISTRICT.

Superintendent Registrar, Christopher Cheesbrough, Front street, Brampton
Registrars of Births & Deaths, Brampton Sub-District, James Dodd; deputy, Frederick W. Cheesbrough; Hayton Sub-District, John W. Steele, Gelt Mill, Hayton; deputy, Mrs. Steele

BRAMPTON. # CUMBERLAND.

PUBLIC OFFICERS.

Certifying Factory Surgeon, James Arnott M.D., B.S., J.P. Rose villa
Clerk to Alston, Longtown & Brampton Sub-Committee, Cumberland Local Pensions Committee, Andrew Warwick, Tree terrace
Clerk to the Commissioners of Taxes, Eskdale Ward Division, James Dodd, Union offices, Union lane
Customs & Excise Officer & Pension Officer for Alston, Longtown & Brampton Sub-Committee, Cumberland Local Pensions Committee, Alfred J. Smith
Main Road Surveyor for Brampton District to the County Council, George A. Gray, 6o Main street
Veterinary Inspector under the Diseases of Animals Acts to the Brampton District & assistant to the County Council, William Toppin Hewetson M.R.C.V.S. Main street

PLACES OF WORSHIP.

St. Martin's Church, Front street, Rev. Edwin Thomas Shepherd B.A. vicar, & surrogate

Presbyterian Church of England, Main street, Rev. Gustavus J. Goodman; seats 220
Primitive Methodist, Moat side, Rev. Stanley King Chesworth; seats 400
Wesleyan Methodist, Main street, Rev. Mark H. Earl

EDUCATIONAL.

Brampton County Secondary School (mixed), opened in 1909, for 88 scholars, now (1928) 120; George Sydney Wood B.Sc. master

CONVEYANCE.

Railway Stations.—Brampton Junction & Naworth (L. & N. E)
Omnibus meets most trains at Brampton junction

CARRIER TO CARLISLE:

Joseph Carruthers, daily, to Back of Market

BRAMPTON.

Marked thus * letters should be addressed Brampton Junction.
PRIVATE RESIDENTS.
(For T N's see general list of Private Residents at end of book.)
Arnott James M.D., J.P. Rose villa
Bell John, Belmore, Station road
Bell Miss, Glendhu, Station road
Bernstein Abraham Lewis M.B., Ch.B. Front st
Burn Pulsford, Tree road
Charlton Miss,2 Milton vils.Station rd
Cheeseman Rev. Thos. Paving brow
Chesworth Rev. Stanley King (Primitive Methodist), Bourne ho.Tree rd
Dickinson John,The Bungalow,Tree rd
Dickinson Mrs. Howglen, Tree road
Dobson William J.P. Howgate, Station road
Earl Rev. Mark H. (Wesleyan Methodist), Wesley manse

Faulkner Charles, Four gables
Fisher C. Wm. Birtle Dene, Tree rd
Goodman Rev. Gustavus J. (Presbyterian), Ashmore
Hallifax F. J., J.P. Oak wood
Harding Misses, Millfield, Lover's la
Harrison George M.B. Glen Ridding, Station road
Harrison William Graham, Leafield
Hetherington Henry, 3 Front street
Hewetson William T. Main street
Jackson Hugh J.P. Green Lane house
James William, The Swarthel
Kimm Alexander Knox,Capontree rd
Lawson Mrs. Westwood, Station road
Lee Mrs. Greenfield
Lee Miss, West hill
Park George, Allenmead, Tree road
Park Joseph, Uplands, Tree road
Richardson John J. Ridge house
Richardson Thomas, Ridge house

Riddell Thomas S. Beech house, Station road
Riddell Tom A. The Glen
Robinson Alfred, Craigmore
Robinson Miss Amy, Croft house
Robinson Johnson, Moss house
Routledge Philip, Craigmore
Shepherd Rev. Edwin Thomas B.A. (vicar & surrogate), St. Martin's vicarage
Smith Edmund Robert, The Knowe
Smith Thomas, Beech house
Sutcliffe Walter, Kirbymoor
Taylor Robert, Milton hall
Thompson Wm. Briggs,Warren bank
Thomson Mrs. 1 Milton villas
Wood George Sidney B.Sc. Ashcroft, Station road
Wotherspoon Mrs. Mayfield, Craw hall
Wrigley Robert, Mansion house

COMMERCIAL.

Early closing day, Thursday.

Marked thus ° farm 150 acres or over.

Abbott Mary (Mrs.), confectioner, Front street
°Adams Rd. Sarginson, farmer, Park barn
Angling Association(Christr. Cheesbrough, sec.),Front st
Armstrong Rt. & Sons, plumbers, Front st
Armstrong Agnes (Mrs.), shopkeeper, Longtown road
Armstrong Archibald, insurance agent, Low Cross street
Armstrong Jacob, plumber, Main st
Armstrong Wm. mineral water mfr. Market pl
Arnott James M.D., B.S.Durh., J.P. surgeon, & medical officer of health & public vaccinator, Brampton union, medical officer of health Brampton Rural Sanitary Authority & to the Poor Law Institution & certifying factory surgeon, Rose villa. T N 21
Askew Thos.Edwd. mngr. of Martins Bank Ltd.Front st
Asti Bros. fried fish dlrs. Front st
Atkinson Wm. & Sons, painters &c. Main st
Atkinson Wm. M. W. saddler & harness mkr. 4 Main st
Baldry Sydney, Bush hotel, Main st
Barnes Robert, saddler, 26 High Cross street
Barron S. dentist, Main street
Batey & Son, mineral water mfrs. Moat side. T N 48
Beaton T. A. The Sands House hotel; accommodation for visitors; garage; cars for hire; all makes of cars & cycles supplied. T N 36
Beaty Tom, haulage contrctr. Railhead. T N 31
Bell Isaac & Son, drapers, 43 Main st
Bell Rt. & Son, fancy repository, Front st
Bell & Thirlwell, agricltrl. implement mkrs. 55 Main st
Bell Thomas Wm. & Joseph, carriage proprs.Falkins hill
Bell Jn. corn & flour mer. Market pl
Bell Mabel (Mrs.), laundress, Nag's Head lane
°Bell Thomas, farmer, Middle farm, Carlisle road
Bell Thos. plumber, Low Cross st
Bell William, Nag's Head hotel, Market place
Bendle Christphr. carman, Gelt rd
Bernstein Abraham Lewis M.B., Ch.B.Glas. surgn.Front st. T N 17
Bird Thomas William, antique dealer, Main street
Blaylock John, butcher, Market place
Bowling Club (Jn. P. Carrick, sec.), Front st
Brampton Agricultural Society (T. W. Watson & J. W. Thomlinson, joint secs)

Brampton Branch British Legion (The Rt. Hon. the Earl of Carlisle J.P. president; C. Porter, hon. sec.), Moat side
Brampton Central Hall (W. G. Harrison, sec.), Main st
Brampton & District Conservative & Unionist Club (Wm. Spooner, sec.), Front st
Brampton Fire Brigade
Brampton Football Club (Thos. Howe, hon. sec)
Brampton Gas Works (John T. Houghton, manager), Carlisle road
Brampton Golf Club (Frank Bell, sec.), Main st
Brampton Liberal Club (Fredk. Vickers, sec.), Main st
Brampton Savings Bank (branch of the Carlisle Savings Bank; established 1818) (Christphr. Cheesbrough, branch mngr.), Market pl.; open from 12.30 to 1.30 p.m. on wednesdays
Brampton Tennis Club (Miss Connie Murray, hon. sec.), Main street
Brampton Total Abstinence Society (W. Jackson, sec)
Brown Wm. & Son, drapers, High Cross st
Brown Fredk. Pilling L.D.S. dental surgn. (attends wed. 10.30 a.m. to 3.30 p.m.), Front st
Burn P. & Son, general drapers, Front street
Burnett J. M. & N. Howard Arms temperance hotel, Front st
Carlisle & North Western Counties Savings Bank (Christphr. Cheesbrough, branch mngr.) (open on wed. 12.30 to 1.30 p.m.), High Cross st
Carlisle South End Co-operative Society Ltd. (No. 8 & 25 branches of), grocers, Front st
Carrick, Riddell & Co. (Tom A. Riddell, sole proprietor), wine & spirit merchants, Main street
Carruthers & Kent, decrtrs. Main st
Carruthers Ellen (Mrs.), confctnr. Carlisle rd
Carruthers Joseph, carrier, Longtown road
Cartmell S. & H. S. solicitors & commissioners for oaths, Main street. T N 2
Cartmell Hy. Studholme, solctr. & commissioner for oaths, clerk to magistrates & registrar of the county court (firm, S. & H. S. Cartmell), Main st
Cheesbrough Christphr. interim supt. registrar,Front st
Cheesbrough T. printer, Front st. T N 43
Clough Rt. coal mer. Longtown rd
Couch Thomas, shoe maker, High Cross street
County Court (His Honor Gawan Taylor LL.B. judge; H.Studholme Cartmell,registrar & acting high bailiff)